My Black Skin

Lebensreisen
A Journey Through Life

Ein Projekt von **Dayan Kodua**
mit Fotos von **Thomas Leidig**

Für Spencer, Sydney Miles, Talisha und Tyrell.

Wir wünschen euch, dass ihr immer nach eurem Talent und Können, eurer Menschlichkeit und Liebe beurteilt werdet und nicht nach Äußerlichkeiten wie eurer Hautfarbe.

Alle Heldinnen und Helden in diesem Buch – und auch die vielen anderen da draußen – arbeiten heute daran. Sie sind aktive Vorbilder und wirken daran mit, dass ihr es in der Zukunft noch besser und leichter haben werdet. So wie andere Heldinnen und Helden bereits vorher den Weg geebnet und frei gemacht haben.

Für alle Eltern, alleinerziehenden Mütter und Väter, aber insbesondere für all die eingewanderten Eltern, die so viel in Kauf genommen haben, um ihren Kindern ein gutes und sicheres Leben zu ermöglichen, und sich bemüht haben, eine neue Sprache zu lernen, sich für eine neue Kultur zu öffnen und sich in die Gesellschaft zu integrieren.

Ihr alle seid Heldinnen und Helden.

Vielen Dank!

For Spencer, Sydney Miles, Talisha and Tyrell.

We wish for you to always be judged by your talent, ability, humanity and love, and not by external factors like the colour of your skin.

All of the heroes in this book – and the many others out there – are working towards this today. They are active role models, helping to make things even better and easier for you in the future – just as other heroes once paved the way for them.

To all parents, including single mothers and fathers, but especially to the immigrant parents who have been through so much to give their children a good, safe life, and who have struggled to learn a new language, open up to a new culture, and integrate into society:

you are all heroes.

Thank you!

Vorwort von Dayan Kodua

Die Würde des Menschen ist unantastbar. Klingt das zu pathetisch?

Rassismus ist ein globales Problem. Aber auch ein deutsches! Der Rassismus ist eines der großen Übel der Menschheit. Die stigmatisierende Ablehnung aufgrund von Hautfarbe und/oder Herkunft zerreißt die Gesellschaft, sie führt zu Ausgrenzung und Gewalt, sie zerstört Menschen und Familien. Dieser Herausforderung muss auf vielen Ebenen mit bürgerlichem Engagement und politischem Willen entschieden begegnet werden. Und ganz pragmatisch gesehen, können wir es uns als Gesellschaft auch nicht leisten, so viele Talente einfach verkümmern zu lassen, nur weil sie nicht dem Klischeebild eines typischen Deutschen entsprechen.

Neben einem breiten Konsens, dass ein rassistisches Weltbild nicht unseren Werten entspricht und nicht entsprechen darf, braucht es Inspiration und vorzeigbare Lebensgeschichten, die uns davon erzählen, wie bereichernd ein vielfältiges Miteinander ist. Vor allem aber braucht es positive Vorbilder von Menschen mit dunkler Hautfarbe, die in Deutschland erfolgreich sind.

Schwarze Deutsche kämpfen leider immer noch dafür, überhaupt »gesehen« zu werden, und sie treffen nach wie vor auf negative Vorurteile. Genau das hat mich motiviert, nach dem ersten Bildband *My Black Skin: Schwarz. Erfolgreich. Deutsch.* im Jahre 2014, noch mehr Vorbilder zeigen zu wollen.

Es geht nicht darum, mit dem Finger auf Menschen zu zeigen, die dieses oder jenes falsch machen. Wichtig ist es, ein anderes, realitätsbezogenes Bild von Schwarzen Deutschen zu zeigen. Das zu zeigen, was wir an Positivem vermitteln können, positive Identifikationsfiguren zu präsentieren. Starke Vorbilder, die mit ihrer persönlichen Erfolgsgeschichte nachhaltigen Eindruck erzeugen, sind die besten Beispiele und ganz sicher Motivation auch für viele jüngere Menschen, egal welchen ethnischen Hintergrund sie haben. Es geht um ein kollektives Miteinander. Und dieses sollte respektvoll und menschlich sein. Dann haben wir als Gesellschaft die Chance, zusammenzuwachsen, Brücken zu bauen und aufeinander zu achten.

Im vorliegenden Bildband *My Black Skin: Lebensreisen* ist jeder einzelne Protagonist eine Heldin oder ein Held auf seine oder ihre Weise.

Und ich freue mich sehr, dass ich auch bei diesem zweiten Band wieder mit so tollen, professionellen und zuverlässigen Menschen zusammenarbeiten durfte, die zu meinen Freunden wurden. Ihr seid das beste Team! Vielen Dank.

Hamburg, im Mai 2022

Foreword by Dayan Kodua

Article 1 of our constitution states that 'human dignity shall be inviolable'.

To some, this might seem melodramatic. Yet while racism is, of course, a global problem, it's also a German one – and it's one of humanity's greatest evils. Stigmatisation and rejection based on skin colour or ethnic background cripple society. They lead to exclusion and violence. And they destroy people and families. Consequently, they present a challenge that we need to meet with decisive civic engagement and political will at every level. From a purely pragmatic point of view, our society can't afford to let so much talent go to waste simply because an individual doesn't fit the mould of a stereotypical German.

Alongside the broad consensus that a racist worldview is not and cannot be reflected in our values, we need inspirational life stories that showcase how enriching life can be in a diverse society. And, above all, we need to see positive role models: people with darker skin who've achieved success in our country.

Unfortunately, Black Germans still struggle to be 'seen' at all and continue to encounter negative bias in their day-to-day lives. This is precisely what inspired me to spotlight another group of trailblazers following the success of my 2014 illustrated book *My Black Skin: Schwarz. Erfolgreich. Deutsch*.

It's not a question of pointing the finger at people who've done this or that wrong. On the contrary, it's about presenting another image of Black Germans that's more grounded in reality. It's important to show what good things we can do and to offer positive representation to those in our community. The best people for the job are strong role models whose success stories can leave a lasting impression on the reader – and who are sure to inspire a great many young people of every race, colour and creed. It's about creating a sense of community that's rooted in humane and respectful co-existence. Only then will we have the opportunity to come together as a society, build bridges, and truly look out for one another.

In this book, *My Black Skin: A Journey Through Life,* each protagonist has demonstrated their own, personal brand of heroism. I'm delighted to have once again had the opportunity to work on this second volume with such wonderful, reliable, consummate professionals, all of whom have become firm friends. You're the best team I could ever ask for – thank you!

Hamburg, May 2022

Vorwort von Dr. Peter Tschentscher

My Black Skin stellt Persönlichkeiten vor, die es in ihrem Leben weit gebracht haben. Sie entwickeln neue medizinische Therapien, führen erfolgreich Unternehmen, betreiben Spitzenforschung, unterrichten an Schulen und Universitäten, schaffen Kultur oder erzielen sportliche Höchstleistungen.

Diese Menschen machen Mut und motivieren. Sie sind ein Vorbild für alle, die noch am Anfang ihres Lebensweges stehen.

Die in diesem Buch dargestellten Lebensläufe sind vielfältig und einzigartig. Alle Personen verbindet, dass sie Schwarze Deutsche sind. Viele von ihnen haben aufgrund ihrer Hautfarbe Diskriminierung und Ausgrenzung erlebt. Sie haben Hürden genommen, die durch Vorurteile entstehen, und ermutigen, sich für Toleranz und Freiheit in unserer Gesellschaft einzusetzen.

Deutschland ist ein internationales Land mit Beziehungen in alle Welt. In Hamburg leben Menschen aus über 180 Staaten. Diese Vielfalt an Kulturen, Religionen und Lebensweisen ist eine Bereicherung und macht das Leben interessant.

Die Porträts und Interviews in diesem Buch zeigen, was diese Frauen und Männer in unsere Gesellschaft einbringen und warum es sich lohnt, sie kennenzulernen.

Ich danke den Beteiligten sehr herzlich für ihren Beitrag zu diesem Projekt und wünsche allen Leserinnen und Lesern viel Freude mit dem zweiten Band von *My Black Skin*.

Dr. Peter Tschentscher
Erster Bürgermeister der Freien und Hansestadt Hamburg

Foreword by Dr. Peter Tschentscher

My Black Skin introduces a group of Germans who have gone far in life. They've developed new medical treatments, run successful businesses, spearheaded high-level research, taught at schools and universities, contributed to our culture, or accomplished fantastic sporting achievements.

These are people who inspire courage and motivation in others. Each of them could be a role model for those just starting their life's journey. And each of the lives and careers depicted in this book are as unique as they are varied.

What connects those interviewed is that they are all Black Germans. Many of them have experienced discrimination and exclusion due to their skin colour. And, in turn, they've overcome the hurdles erected by prejudice and strived to champion tolerance and freedom in our society.

Germany is an international country with links to nations all around the world. Hamburg, alone, is home to people from 180 countries. This wealth of cultures, religions and ways of life enriches us all and makes life interesting.

The portraits and interviews in this book show what these women and men contribute to our society and why it's worth getting to know them.

I'd like to extend my heartfelt thanks to all of the participants for their contributions to this project and hope that every reader enjoys this second volume in the *My Black Skin* series.

Dr Peter Tschentscher
First Mayor of the Free and Hanseatic City of Hamburg

»Ein Held oder eine Heldin ist eine Person, die trotz Schwäche, Zweifeln oder obwohl sie nicht immer die Lösung eines Problems kennt, vorangeht und trotzdem obsiegt.«

"A hero is someone who, in spite of weakness, doubt or not always knowing the answers, goes ahead and overcomes anyway."

Christopher Reeve

Gloria Boateng

LEHRERIN UND MODERATORIN

»Ich glaube an das Gute im Menschen, daran, dass wir Dinge positiv beeinflussen können, wenn wir wollen!«

»Alles, was ich in meinem Leben gemacht habe, kam zufällig auf mich zu«, sagt Gloria Boateng. Es müssen eine Menge glücklicher Zufälle gewesen sein. 1979 in einem Dorf in Ghana in einfache Verhältnisse hineingeboren, ist Boateng heute Lehrerin an einer Stadtteilschule, Moderatorin, Fitnesstrainerin und Ernährungsberaterin. Sie hat ihre Autobiografie geschrieben und ist Vorsitzende eines Vereins. Ihren facettenreichen Werdegang verdankt Boateng wohl eher einer Kombination aus Ehrgeiz und einer großen Portion Selbstvertrauen, garniert mit Zufällen.

Mit zehn Jahren kommt sie nach Deutschland, wohin ihre Mutter und ihr Großvater zuvor schon übergesiedelt waren. Die Mutter wird abgeschoben. Der Großvater ist es, von dem sie zum ersten Mal im Leben Liebe und Geborgenheit erfährt. Jedoch stirbt er ein Jahr nach ihrer Ankunft in dem ihr noch fremden Land. Pflegeeltern nehmen sich ihrer an. Zu ihrem zwölfjährigen Ich würde sie aus heutiger Sicht sagen: »Schau, was du bis hierhin alles geschafft hast. Du hast viel Kraft in dir, und eine höhere Kraft um dich herum hilft dir, all das zu schaffen, wofür du dich anstrengst. Also steh auf und mach weiter. Geh weiter deinen Weg. Du wirst dort ankommen, wo du hinwillst. Vielleicht mit Umwegen, aber du wirst es schaffen. Das Leben meint es nämlich gut mit dir.«

Wenn Boateng heute Rückschau hält auf das, was sie geschafft hat, sehe sie, was sie noch schaffen könne, sagt sie. Es ist der Blick auf das Leben einer Frau, die sich früh bewusst ist, dass die besten Chancen auf soziale und wirtschaftliche Teilhabe hat, wer über Bildung verfügt. Und so wehrt sie sich auch gegen die Hauptschulempfehlung ihrer Lehrkräfte und wechselt auf eine Gesamtschule. Dort macht sie Abitur und bekommt kurz darauf ein Kind. Während die Tochter in einer Kita betreut wird, absolviert sie eine Ausbildung zur Fremdsprachenkorrespondentin, die sie aufgrund ihrer guten Kenntnisse in Englisch und Französisch um ein Jahr verkürzen kann. Die Universität Hamburg wird anschließend ihr Arbeitgeber. Als eine Professorin sie fragt, ob sie sich vorstellen könne, als Lehrbeauftragte an einer Schule Fremdsprachen zu unterrichten, sagt sie zu. Damals gibt es einen Mangel an Lehrkräften mit diesen Fächern, und so hilft sie über mehrere Jahre immer mal wieder an unterschiedlichen Schulen aus. Dabei merkt sie, dass ihr das Unterrichten liegt und sie auch mit schwierigen Kindern und Jugendlichen gut zurechtkommt.

Die sportliche junge Frau, die als Jugendliche Leistungssport betrieben hatte, beschließt daraufhin, auf Lehramt zu studieren. Eine Entscheidung, die sie trotz manch schwierigem Moment mit Eltern, Schulleitungen, dem System Schule und den oft ungünstigen Rahmenbedingungen der Arbeit nie bereut hat. Boateng: »Ich kann ständig meine Kompetenzen erweitern, trage zwar den Titel Lehrerin, bin aber die in der Klasse,

TEACHER AND PRESENTER

"I believe that people are fundamentally good – and that we can choose to have a positive impact on the world!"

"Everything I've done in my life I owe to serendipity and happy accidents," says Gloria Boateng. It must have been a whole lot of happy accidents. Born in 1979 into a modest home in a Ghanaian village, Boateng is now a teacher at a German district school, a presenter, fitness trainer and food coach, has penned her autobiography, and is the chair of an education association. Boateng credits her varied career to a large dollop of ambition and self-confidence, seasoned with a string of lucky breaks.

She arrived in Germany at the age of ten, joining her mother and grandfather who'd already settled there. However, her mother would later be deported. As a result, Boateng's grandfather was the first person in her life who gave her genuine love and security. Unfortunately, he died a year after her arrival in this still-foreign land, so the little girl was therefore taken in by foster parents. What would she say to her twelve-year-old self today? "Look at what you've achieved so far. You have a deep well of inner strength and a higher power all around you that will help you to achieve everything you're striving for. So get up and keep going. Carry on your way and you'll get to where you want to go. It may take a few detours, but you can do it – because life has good things in store for you."

When Boateng looks back on what she's accomplished today, she only sees how much there's left to do. This is the mindset of a woman who realised early on in life that the best opportunities for social and economic participation lie in education. For this reason, she challenged her teachers' recommendations that she attend lower secondary school and switched to a comprehensive, where she completed her school-leaving certificate. Shortly thereafter, she had her first child. While her daughter was at nursery school, she trained as a foreign language correspondent, shaving a year off of her course time thanks to her excellent knowledge of English and French. She then went on to be employed by the University of Hamburg. When a professor asked if she had ever thought about teaching foreign languages, she decided to give it a try. There was a shortage of language teaching staff at the time, so Boateng supported classes at a variety of schools over the years. During this period, she realised that she enjoyed teaching and got along well with 'difficult' children and youths.

The sporty young woman, who'd spent her youth as a competitive athlete, therefore decided to study to become a qualified teacher. It was a decision that led to difficult moments with parents, school administrations and the education system, often in unfavourable working conditions, but she never regretted it. Boateng says: "I can continually broaden my skills. I may be the teacher, but it's me who

die am meisten lernt. Lehrkräfte sind in so vielen Bereichen gefordert, lösungsorientiert zu denken – sozial, emotional, psychologisch und didaktisch.« Dabei, so sagt sie, würden ihr die ersten zehn Jahre ihres Lebens in Ghana helfen. »Ich habe in meiner Kindheit eine andere Herangehensweise an verschiedene Situationen erfahren und bin nicht so sehr auf Probleme fokussiert. In dem Ghana meiner Kindheit steht man nach Niederlagen einfach wieder auf und macht weiter. Ich bin dankbar, dass mich diese Sichtweise geprägt hat.« Diese Erfahrung hilft Boateng auch nach ihrer Scheidung und ganz besonders im Umgang mit rassistischen Angriffen. »Ich habe viel Erniedrigung, Beschimpfungen und körperliche Gewalt erlebt und hatte aufgrund dessen Krankenhausaufenthalte.« Auch den institutionellen Rassismus in Unternehmen und Schulen erlebt sie. »Dabei hätte ich gedacht, das Land verändert sich durch Migrationsprozesse und die wachsende Vielfalt«, so Boateng. An Schwarzer Hautfarbe, so Boateng, entzünde sich das Bedürfnis vieler Menschen nach Kategorisierung, Ausgrenzung und insbesondere nach Privilegierung beziehungsweise Entmachtung. Sie selbst dagegen verbinde mit ihrer Herkunft ein (vergleichsweise) friedliches Zusammenleben von Menschen aus vielen unterschiedlichen Volksgemeinschaften mit unterschiedlichen Kulturen, die viele verschiedene Sprachen sprechen, und mit ihrer Hautfarbe verbindet sie eine »Steh wieder auf«-Mentalität – und die Sonne.

Der Glaube an eine höhere Kraft und die vom Großvater erfahrene liebevolle Fürsorge verhindern, dass die Lehrerin aufgrund negativer Erfahrungen ein negatives Menschenbild entwickelt – ganz im Gegenteil: »Ich liebe Menschen und respektiere sie.« Sie selbst gehe mit anderen nicht zu streng ins Gericht und habe mit dieser Einstellung frühe Kindheitsprägungen hinter sich gelassen, denn ihr Elternhaus sei sehr strafend gewesen, und auch in der Grundschule in Ghana seien Schläge zur damaligen Zeit normal gewesen. »Ich habe gelernt, dass Fehler dazu da sind, gemacht, aber nicht ständig wiederholt zu werden. Besonders die, die anderen wehtun. Ich nutze Fehler, um mein Verhalten zu reflektieren.« Sie schätze es sehr, wenn sich jemand für einen Fehler aufrichtig entschuldigen könne. »Das habe auch ich gelernt.« Doch nicht immer lässt sie sich von der Ratio leiten, sagt vielmehr über sich: »Es erstaunt mich, dass ich immer noch so ein impulsiver Kindskopf bin.« Sie beschreibt sich selbst als eine Person, die gern situativ lacht und sich darüber freut, wenn fremde Menschen ihr ein Lächeln schenken, zum Beispiel in der S-Bahn. Ob dort, in der Schule oder im Sportverein, wo sie Kurse gibt, ist die Hobbyköchin dankbar für zwischenmenschliche Begegnungen, »für die Energie, die ich in mir trage, für die Liebe, die ich bekomme, und das privilegierte Leben, das ich führen darf. Meine Dankbarkeit dafür ist grenzenlos.«

Schon früh möchte sie der Gesellschaft etwas zurückgeben und gründet deshalb als Studentin mit anderen Studierenden den gemeinnützigen Verein SchlauFox. Die haupt- und ehrenamtlichen Mitglieder stehen benachteiligten Kindern unterstützend zur Seite. Viele von ihnen haben wie sie selbst und ihr vierjähriges Pflegekind ebenfalls Wurzeln in einem anderen Land. Vorbilder, Heldinnen oder Helden kann die Vereinsvorsitzende nicht nennen. Aber von ihrem vorbildlichen Engagement nimmt 2019 sogar der Bundespräsident Notiz und verleiht ihr das Bundesverdienstkreuz. Mit Zufall hat das rein gar nichts zu tun.

learns the most in the classroom. Teachers are challenged to be solution-oriented in so many areas – socially, emotionally, psychologically and pedagogically." This is something she believes her ten years in Ghana helped with. "During my childhood, I experienced different approaches to different situations, and I don't tend to get stuck on problems. When you experienced failure in the Ghana of my childhood, you simply got up and kept going. I'm very grateful for the ways this perspective has shaped me." This experience also helped Boateng after her divorce, and especially in dealing with racist attacks: "I've experienced a lot of humiliation, abuse and physical violence, and have even been hospitalised because of it." She's also experienced institutional racism at schools and in the business world: "I'd have thought that the country is changing now thanks to migration and growing diversity," says Boateng. The educator feels that Black skin ignites a need in many people to categorise and exclude – and, most notably, to privilege and disempower. She, on the other hand, associates her heritage with the (comparatively) peaceful coexistence of people from many different communities with different cultures and speaking many different languages. She associates her skin colour with a "get up again" mentality – and with sun.

Her belief in a higher power and the loving care she received from her grandfather have prevented the teacher's negative experiences from giving her a negative view of humanity – quite the opposite: "I love people and respect them." She isn't overly harsh with others, and has thus turned away from her early childhood conditioning; her parental home was very punitive and beatings were considered normal even in primary school in Ghana: "I've learnt that mistakes happen, but shouldn't be constantly repeated – especially if they hurt others. I use mistakes to reflect on my behaviour." She really values when someone can sincerely apologise for their mistakes: "This is something else I learnt." But she doesn't always let herself be guided by reason, explaining: "It amazes me that I'm still such an impulsive child!" She describes herself as a person who enjoys spontaneous laughter and delights in strangers giving her a smile on the train, for instance. Whether at school or the sports club where she runs courses, the amateur chef is grateful for her interpersonal relationships, "for the energy I hold inside me, for the love I receive, and for the privileged life I get to lead. My gratitude for these things is endless."

Boateng knew at an early age that she wanted to give something back, and this is why she founded the SchlauFox ("clever fox") non-profit association with her fellow students. The association's full-time and volunteer members provide one-to-one assistance to disadvantaged children. Many of them, like Boateng and her four-year-old foster child, also have roots in other countries. As chairwoman of the association, Boateng can't name any role models or heroes. Nevertheless, even the German Federal President has taken note of her admirable work, awarding her the Order of Merit of the Federal Republic of Germany in 2019. And that had nothing at all to do with serendipity.

Samuel Agyapong

MAURER

»Ich glaube, dass man seine Ziele im Leben erreichen kann, wenn man nur fest genug daran glaubt.«

Samuel Agyapong ist überwältigt, als er kurz vor Weihnachten 2020 endlich die Urkunde in den Händen hält: Die Handwerkskammer hat seine Kenntnisse und beruflichen Erfahrungen als Maurer anerkannt, wie es das 2012 in Kraft getretene Berufsqualifizierungsgesetz vorsieht. Mit diesem Zertifikat ist er jedem in Deutschland ausgebildeten Maurer gleichgestellt, darf die gleichen Maschinen bedienen und erhält den gleichen Lohn. »Manchmal kann ich es noch immer nicht fassen, dass ich es tatsächlich geschafft habe«, sagt er heute stolz. Fast drei Jahre habe das Verfahren gedauert, erzählt der Vater einer Tochter im Kindergartenalter. Gefragt waren Ausdauer und Beharrlichkeit. »Man schafft es hier nur, wenn man es wirklich ernst meint und am Ball bleibt.«

In der ghanaischen Millionenmetropole Kumasi lernt Samuel Agyapong bereits als Kind die Härten des Lebens kennen. Er wächst mit drei Schwestern bei Mutter und Großmutter auf. Sein Vater, ein Staatsangestellter, hatte die Familie früh verlassen. Die Geschwister gehen zur Schule, müssen jedoch bald mit anpacken, weil das Geld nicht reicht. Seit seinem zehnten Geburtstag hilft Samuel der Mutter jeden Tag nach Schulschluss an ihrem Marktstand, wo sie Leder, Zangen und anderen Schuhmacherbedarf verkaufen. Er liebt Fußball und Actionfilme, doch für beides fehlt oft die Zeit. Nach neun Jahren Schule absolviert Agyapong ein Praktikum auf dem Bau und findet einen Job in einer kleinen Baufirma. Doch der Lohn kommt nur unregelmäßig. »Wenn wir keinen Auftrag hatten, half ich meiner Mutter auf dem Markt«, erinnert er sich an diese Zeit. Als ein Bekannter dem jungen Mann die Möglichkeit eröffnet, Ghana in Richtung Europa zu verlassen, ergreift Samuel Agyapong die Chance. Mit einem kleinen Koffer und voller Hoffnung auf ein besseres Leben besteigt er im Februar 2014 ein Flugzeug, das ihn ins norwegische Oslo bringt. Sein Weg führt ihn weiter in die Niederlande, wo er eine deutsche Frau kennenlernt. Als sie ein Kind von ihm erwartet, kann er einen Antrag auf Familienzusammenführung stellen. Ein knappes Jahr muss er in einer tristen Aufnahmeeinrichtung im mecklenburgischen Horst ausharren, bis er die Erlaubnis erhält, zu Freundin und Tochter nach Hamburg zu ziehen. Immerhin nutzt Samuel Agyapong die Zeit, um Deutsch zu lernen.

Dass er in Deutschland Arbeit als Maurer finden wird, davon wagt der junge Handwerker nicht mal zu träumen. »Ich war zu jedem Job bereit«, sagt Agyapong rückblickend. Trotz der schwierigen Bedingungen macht ihm seine Arbeit immer Spaß: »Ich bin gut in Zeichnen und Rechnen, und es gefällt mir, immer wieder neue Projekte und neue Herausforderungen zu haben. Jeder Tag ist anders!« Sein Arbeitsvermittler vom Jobcenter überzeugt ihn, bei der Handwerkskammer die Anerkennung seiner beruflichen Qualifikation zu beantragen. »Das Verfahren ist kompliziert, und ich war nicht sicher, ob ich es schaffen würde«, erzählt Agyapong.

BRICKLAYER

"I believe you can achieve your goals in life if you just believe in them hard enough."

When he finally held his certificate in his hands shortly before Christmas 2020, Samuel Agyapong felt overwhelmed; the Chamber of Skilled Trades had recognised his knowledge and professional experience as a bricklayer, as required by the German Vocational Qualifications Act 2012. With this certificate, he was considered the equal of any bricklayer trained in Germany, allowing him to operate the same machinery and receive the same wage. "Sometimes I still can't believe that I actually made it," says Agyapong proudly. The father of one explains that the process took almost three years – and demanded perseverance and persistence: "You can only make it here if you take things seriously and keep your eye on the ball."

Agyapong became acquainted with life's hardships during his childhood in the Ghanaian metropolis of Kumasi. He was raised with his three sisters by his mother and grandmother. His father, a state employee, had long since abandoned the family. The siblings went to school, but soon had to contribute to the household because the family didn't have enough money. From his tenth birthday onwards, Agyapong helped his mother every day after school at their market stall, where they sold leather, pliers and other shoemaking supplies. He loved football and action films, but there was rarely time for either. After nine years of school, Agyapong completed a traineeship in construction and found a job with a small construction company. However, his pay was erratic. "When we didn't have a contract to fulfil, I helped my mother at the market," he recalls. When an acquaintance offered the young man the opportunity to leave Ghana for Europe, Agyapong seized his chance. Armed with a small suitcase and filled with hope for a better life, he boarded a plane in February 2014 to Oslo, Norway. His journey continued to the Netherlands, where he met a German woman. When she became pregnant, he was able to apply for a family reunification visa. He had to wait out a year in a dreary reception centre in Horst, Mecklenburg, before he received permission to move in with his girlfriend and daughter in Hamburg, so Agyapong used this time to learn German.

Back then, the young tradesman didn't dare to dream that he would find work as a bricklayer in Germany. "I was prepared to do any job," he says. Despite the difficult working conditions, he's always enjoyed his work: "I'm good at drawing and arithmetic, and I like always having new projects and challenges to work on. Every day is different!" It was his job centre advisor who convinced him to apply to the Chamber of Skilled Trades for recognition of his professional qualifications. "The procedure is complicated and I wasn't sure if I'd be able to do it," Agyapong admits. He was therefore glad to have the support of a Chamber of Skilled Trades employee.

Er sei froh gewesen, dass ihn eine Mitarbeiterin der Handwerkskammer unterstützt habe.

Wieder heißt es warten. Sieben Monate dauert es, bis seine Mutter die Schulzeugnisse und Arbeitsbescheinigungen in Ghana eingeholt und nach Hamburg geschickt hat. Dann folgt eine dreitägige Prüfung. Agyapong: »Ich musste zeigen, dass ich mauern, verputzen und verschalen kann.« Er kann die Prüfer überzeugen, doch fehlen ihm noch spezielle Kenntnisse über Brandschutz und Wärmedämmung, die nur in Deutschland vermittelt werden. Die eignet sich Samuel Agyapong während eines einjährigen Praktikums bei seinem heutigen Arbeitgeber an. Die kleine Hamburger Baufirma ist auf Renovierungsarbeiten spezialisiert.

Zum Durchhalten habe ihn stets der Gedanke an seine Mutter ermutigt, die er als seine persönliche Heldin bezeichnet. Agyapong: »Sie hat alles für uns Kinder getan. An sich selbst hat sie nie gedacht.« Es sei ihr schwergefallen, den einzigen Sohn nach Europa ziehen zu lassen. Dennoch habe sie ihn bestärkt, in der Fremde sein Glück zu versuchen. »Es war mein fester Wille, mir in Deutschland ein neues Leben aufzubauen«, sagt der gläubige junge Mann. »Von hier aus kann ich sie besser unterstützen.« Die Entscheidung, seine Heimat zu verlassen, würde er immer wieder treffen. Jedoch bereue er, nicht früher gegangen zu sein. »Für Jugendliche gibt es hier viele Möglichkeiten«, so Agyapong. »Wenn ich mit 18 Jahren nach Deutschland gekommen wäre, hätte ich nach der Maurerausbildung eine zweite Ausbildung zum Fliesenleger machen können.«

Bei seiner Arbeit auf Baustellen in ganz Norddeutschland lernt Samuel Agyapong sehr unterschiedliche Menschen kennen. Stets sei er respektvoll behandelt worden. Umso mehr habe ihn kürzlich ein rassistisches Erlebnis erschüttert: Als er im Haus eines Kunden Wände verputzt, füllt dieser gerade Futter für seinen Hund ab. Agyapong: »Plötzlich, aus dem Nichts, hat er mir das Hundefutter vor die Nase gehalten.« Der Maurer erstarrt, doch dann verputzt er mechanisch weiter. »Ich habe gelächelt, damit ich nicht böse werde«, erinnert er sich an die Erniedrigung. »Sonst hätte ich vielleicht etwas Schlechtes getan.«

Überhaupt sind ihm die Deutschen zunächst sehr fremd. »Die Kollegen waren sehr zurückhaltend. Ich dachte, sie wollen keine Freundschaft mit mir schließen«, erzählt Samuel Agyapong. »Dann wurde mir klar, dass sie sich Zeit gegeben haben, um mich besser kennenzulernen.« Auch er versuche, die Menschen und ihre Kultur kennenzulernen und sich den Gepflogenheiten anzupassen.

Von seiner Freundin lebt Samuel Agyapong mittlerweile getrennt. An den Wochenenden holt er seine Tochter ab und geht mit ihr spazieren oder auf den Spielplatz. Danach besucht er den Gottesdienst. Actionfilme liebt er noch immer. Nun hat er genug Zeit, um sich diese zu Hause auf dem Sofa anzuschauen. Auf seinen bisherigen Lebensweg zurückblickend, würde er seinem zwölfjährigen Ich mit folgenden Worten Mut zusprechen: »Du musst hart und diszipliniert arbeiten und fest entschlossen sein. Dann schaffst du es, genug zum Leben zu verdienen und deine Familie zu unterstützen.«

Once again, he found himself playing a waiting game; it took seven months for his mother to collect his school reports and work certificates in Ghana and send them to Hamburg. Then came a three-day examination. "I had to show that I can lay bricks, plaster and board up," Agyapong describes. He convinced the examiners, but still lacked specific knowledge of fire safety and heat insulation, which was only taught in Germany. The expert bricklayer therefore plugged the gaps in his knowledge during a one-year traineeship with his current employer, a small Hamburg construction company specialising in renovation work.

He was always encouraged to persevere by the thought of his mother, whom he describes as his personal hero: "She did everything for us kids. She never gave a thought to herself." It was difficult for her to let her only son move to Europe. Nevertheless, she encouraged him to try his luck in a foreign country. "It was my firm intention to build a new life in Germany," says the devout young man, "I can support her better from here." If he had the chance, he'd make the same decision again. However, he regrets that he didn't arrive earlier: "There are many opportunities for young people here. If I'd come to Germany when I was eighteen, I could've done a second apprenticeship as a tiler after training as a bricklayer."

In his work on construction sites throughout northern Germany, Agyapong gets to know people from all walks of life. He's always been treated with respect, so he was all the more shocked by a recent racist incident. While he was plastering walls in a customer's house, the customer set out some food for his dog: "Suddenly, out of nowhere, the customer shoved the dog food under my nose." The bricklayer froze, and then continued with his plastering on autopilot. "I smiled so that I wouldn't get angry," he says, recalling the humiliation, "otherwise I might have done something I'd regret."

In general, German people seemed very foreign to him at first. "My colleagues were very reserved. I thought they didn't want to make friends with me," shares Agyapong. "Then I realised that they were just giving themselves time to get to know me better." Likewise, the builder tried to get to know the people and their culture and to adapt to local customs.

Today, Agyapong has separated from his girlfriend. At the weekend, he picks up his toddler daughter and takes her for a walk or to the playground. Afterwards, he attends a church service. He still loves action films – and now he has time to enjoy them at home on his sofa. Looking back on his life's journey so far, he would offer his twelve-year-old self these words of encouragement: "You have to work hard and be disciplined and determined. Then you'll be able to earn enough to live on and support your family."

Prof. Dr. Marylyn Addo

INFEKTIOLOGIN

»Ich glaube an die Wissenschaft und an Fakten.«

20 Jahre lang kämpfte sie gegen das Human Immunodeficiency Virus (HI-Virus), später gegen den Ebola-Erreger und in der Pandemie 2020/2021 gegen das Sars-Coronavirus-2. Als Antrieb nennt Prof. Dr. med. Marylyn Addo dabei den Wunsch, »dass die Welt ein gesünderer, besserer Ort wird«. Die Leiterin der Sektion Infektiologie am Universitätskrankenhaus Eppendorf (UKE) ist durch ihre Forschungsarbeit an Covid-19 und der damit einhergehenden intensiven Berichterstattung durch die Medien einer breiten Öffentlichkeit bekannt geworden. Wenn sie über ihren Beruf spricht, ist jedoch deutlich herauszuhören, wie wichtig ihr die Arbeit im Team ist: »Ich freue mich, wenn meine Mentees einen Meilenstein erreicht haben. Die Erfolge meiner talentierten jungen Mitarbeiterinnen und Mitarbeiter machen mich stolz.« Ihren Wissensdurst und ihre Neugier konnte sich die Professorin auch nach vielen Jahren wissenschaftlichen Arbeitens im In- und Ausland erhalten, denn dabei könne sie »spannenden und wichtigen Fragen nachgehen«. Oft ist es Pionierarbeit, wie bei der Entwicklung eines neuen Impfstoffs.

Die 1970 in Bonn als Tochter einer Deutschen und eines Ghanaers geborene Forscherin, die mit ihrem sieben Jahre jüngeren Bruder im nordrhein-westfälischen Troisdorf aufwächst, hat eine Leidenschaft für das Kunstturnen und ist in der katholischen Gemeinde aktiv. »Der Kaplan hat uns Jugendliche motiviert, uns zu engagieren. Ich war Gruppenleiterin und habe im Jugendchor gesungen.« Diese Erfahrungen prägen die junge Frau, die im Grunde ihres Herzens schon damals Medizin studieren will, wären da nur nicht die vielfältigen anderen Interessen und Begabungen, die der Jugendlichen die Berufswahl schwer machen. »Ich habe alles abgeklopft, was ich sonst noch hätte machen können. Mich interessierten Theologie, Sport, Lebensmittelchemie, und auch Philosophie habe ich mir ernsthaft angeschaut.« Bereits vor dem Abi ist dann aber die Entscheidung für das Medizinstudium gefallen. Kinderneurochirurgie und Gynäkologie/Geburtsheilkunde finden zunächst ihr Interesse.

»Bei einem Auslandsjahr in Frankreich 1992 habe ich dann Feuer gefangen für die Infektiologie.« Eigentlich sollte sie dort ein Praktikum in Kinderheilkunde absolvieren, doch »das passte weder für die eine noch für die andere Seite«, erinnert sie sich. In der Abteilung für das damals noch wenig erforschte HIV dagegen ist noch ein Platz frei. Addo findet Gefallen an der Pionierarbeit, nicht zuletzt, weil die Beschäftigung mit dem Virus eine weitere Dimension als die bloße biologische hat: »Die Erkrankten hatten oft viele Ängste. Außerdem war die Erkrankung häufig mit Stigmatisierung verbunden, und ich war als Ärztin oft die Einzige, der sich die Patienten anvertrauten.« In dieser Zeit nimmt sie an vielen Beerdigungen teil. »Das hat mich belastet«, gibt sie zu. Die gemachten Erfahrungen motivieren die Studentin, ihre Doktorarbeit in der Schweiz über HIV zu schreiben. »Ich wollte einen Beitrag leisten, um dieses Problem zu lösen.« Ihr Forschergeist und die Identifikation mit den Betroffenen bringen sie dazu, die Tabletten für die Patienten selbst auszuprobieren, um die Nebenwirkungen am eigenen Körper zu spüren. 20 Jahre soll die

VIROLOGIST

"I believe in science and facts."

She battled against the human immunodeficiency virus (HIV) for 20 years. Next, she was pitted against the Ebola virus. And then, most recently, she took on SARS coronavirus 2 in the 2020/2021 pandemic. Professor Marylyn Addo is a woman driven by the desire to "make the world a better, healthier place". The head of the Infectious Diseases Unit at the University Medical Center Hamburg-Eppendorf (UKE) has become a familiar face to the wider public through her research on Covid-19 and the accompanying intense media coverage. When she talks about her job, however, it's clear just how important teamwork is to her: "I'm delighted when my mentees reach a milestone. I'm very proud of my talented young colleagues' achievements." Even after many years of scientific work at home and abroad, the professor has retained her curiosity and thirst for knowledge because, in doing so, she's able to "answer important, intriguing questions". Very often, her work is pioneering – such as the development of a new vaccine.

Born in Bonn in 1970 to a German mother and a Ghanaian father, the researcher grew up in Troisdorf, North Rhine-Westphalia, with a brother seven years her junior. In her youth, the future doctor developed a passion for artistic gymnastics and was a practising Catholic: "The chaplain encouraged us youngsters to get involved in the community. I was a group leader and also sang in the youth choir." These experiences shaped the young woman; in her heart of hearts, she wanted to study medicine even then, yet had many other interests and talents that made it difficult for the teenager to choose a career: "I ticked off everything else I could have done. I was interested in theology, sports, food chemistry, and even took a serious look at philosophy." Nevertheless, she made the decision to study medicine before she'd even finished secondary school.

Initially, she was drawn to paediatric neurosurgery and gynaecology/obstetrics. "It was during my year abroad in France in 1992 that I took a shine to infectious diseases." She was actually supposed to complete an internship in paediatrics while abroad, but recalls that "it didn't work out one way or another". Meanwhile, there was still a place available at the HIV clinic – focusing on a disease that was still poorly researched at the time. Addo enjoyed the pioneering nature of the work, not least because dealing with this virus went beyond the biological: "The sufferers often had a lot of fears and the disease carried a heavy stigma. As a doctor, I was often the only one in whom patients confided." She attended a great many funerals during this time, something she admits "weighed on her". These experiences motivated the student to write her doctoral thesis in Switzerland on the subject of HIV: "I wanted to contribute to solving the problem." Her spirit of research and identification with those affected led her to try out patients' tablets for herself, just so she could feel their side effects on her own body. Addo's study of the virus and the diseases

Beschäftigung mit dem Virus und den Krankheiten, die es auslöst, schließlich andauern, doch das weiß sie noch nicht, als sie nach ihrer Dissertation zunächst eine Weiterbildung in Tropenmedizin in London belegen will. Sie ergattert ein Stipendium, und so wird daraus ein einjähriger Masterkurs.

Rückblickend sagt Addo: »Ich bin für sehr viele Dinge dankbar. Für meine Familie, Freunde, Gesundheit, einen Beruf, der Berufung ist, und für die Möglichkeiten, die ich hatte. Die muss man natürlich auch ergreifen.« Es gibt auch Zeiten, in denen die Wissenschaftlerin, mittlerweile mit Lebensmittelpunkt in Boston, »dreimal pro Woche alles hinwerfenn« will. Zu aufreibend ist der Spagat zwischen Forschungslabor und dem Familienleben mit zwei Kindern. »In dieser Zeit war ich immer müde und hatte das Gefühl, ich mache meine Arbeit nicht gut genug. Man kann immer noch ein Papier lesen, noch ein Experiment machen, wenn man nicht um 9 Uhr seine Kinder in die Kita bringt und sie gegen 17 Uhr dort wieder abholt.« In den 14 Jahren, die sie in den USA verbringt, hilft ihr die gute Infrastruktur bei der Arbeit und die Gemeinschaft der »Working Mom Group«, ihr tägliches Pensum zu schaffen. Prägend für ihre Arbeitsweise als spätere Führungskraft wird in dieser Zeit der Führungsstil ihres Mentors und Laborchefs Bruce Walker. »Bruce hat immer Leute aus verschiedenen Sparten zusammengebracht und das Miteinander gefördert. Das versuche ich seitdem auch.«

Später, sie erforscht gerade das 2014 und 2015 in westafrikanischen Staaten grassierende Ebola-Virus, stößt sie abermals an ihre Grenzen. Im Rückblick auf diese arbeitsreiche Zeit sagt sie: »Mir ist die Batterie leergelaufen.« Addo steuert dagegen, indem sie an einem Resilienztraining teilnimmt. Mittlerweile geht die Abteilungsleiterin zum Coaching

it causes would ultimately continue for 20 years, but she didn't yet know that when she first became interested in studying tropical medicine in London – having been awarded a scholarship allowing her to complete a one-year master's course there.

Looking back, Addo says: "I'm very grateful for many things. For my family, friends and health, for a profession that's truly my calling, and for all the opportunities I was given. Of course, you have to take them." The research scientist, next based in Boston, admits there were periods when she wanted to "toss everything aside three times a week". The balancing act between her research lab and her family life with two children could be gruelling: "At the time, I was always tired and felt like I wasn't doing my job well enough. You can always read one more paper or do one more experiment – if you don't take your kids to nursery at 9am and pick them up around 5pm." In the fourteen years she spent in the US, she says the good infrastructure at work and the community offered by the local 'Working Mom Group' helped her to manage her daily workload. The leadership style of her mentor and lab head, Bruce Walker, was formative to her approach as a future leader: "Bruce always brought together people from various disciplines and encouraged cooperation, and that's what I've been trying to do ever since."

Later, when she was researching the Ebola virus running rampant in West Africa in 2014 and 2015, Addo hit a wall again. When she looks back on this time in her life, she says: "My batteries were completely empty." She countered this by undergoing resilience training. Since then, the department head has received executive coaching and meditates daily: "Work is always too much. You have to accept that

für Führungskräfte und meditiert täglich. »Die Arbeit ist immer zu viel. Man muss aushalten, dass man oft nicht alles schaffen kann. Das ist manchmal das Anstrengendste an der Tätigkeit.« Zum Ausgleich ist sie in ihrer Freizeit gern in der Natur unterwegs, hat Spaß an Karten- und Brettspielen und verbringt Zeit mit Partner, Familie und Freunden. Auch ihr Humor ist ein Ventil zum Abbau von Spannungen: »Ich lache gern, zum Beispiel über Witze, gut gemachte Comedy oder auch über mich selbst.«

Wenn sie eine Sache anders machen könnte, dann wäre das, Dinge entspannter anzugehen, sich selbst nicht zu sehr unter Druck zu setzen. Das möchte sie auch als Mentorin ihren Schützlingen vermitteln. »Ich sage ihnen: ›Sieh doch mal, was du schon alles geschafft hast.‹« Wichtig ist der Infektiologin auch eine offene Fehlerkultur, die es in der von ihr geleiteten Abteilung gebe. »Fehler sind etwas Wichtiges, solange man aus ihnen lernt. Keiner sollte Angst haben, etwas falsch zu machen. Das heißt aber nicht, dass man nicht sorgfältig sein sollte, und man sollte keinen Fehler zweimal machen«, so die Fußball-Begeisterte.

Addo sagt, sie sei mit vielen Freiheiten und dennoch sehr behütet aufgewachsen, mit Ballettunterricht und Musikschule. Heute sieht sie das Aufwachsen in zwei Kulturen als Reichtum an, aber als Kind will sie auf keinen Fall auffallen. »Das war lange mein größter Wunsch.« Nicht aufzufallen als Schwarze, ist schwer in einer mittelgroßen Stadt mit kaum anderen Schwarzen Familien im Stadtteil. Das ist auch der Grund, warum sie manchmal nicht will, dass ihr Vater zum Elternabend geht. Doch vor rassistisch motivierten Vorfällen kann auch das behütetste Elternhaus nicht schützen. Einmal ist Hundekot an die Garage der Familie geschmiert, ein anderes Mal wird ihr Freund rassistisch beschimpft. Addo dazu: »Ausgrenzung erfolgt aufgrund von Herkunft, nicht nur von Hautfarbe. Ich fühle mich wohl in meiner Haut. Und meine Kinder wachsen in einer Welt auf, die relativ divers ist.«

Ghana, die Heimat ihres Vaters, besucht sie oft und hat die Kultur auch ihren Kindern nahegebracht. Durch berufliche Aufenthalte kennt sie auch Botswana, Uganda und Südafrika. Für den südafrikanischen Freiheitskämpfer und ehemaligen Präsidenten Nelson Mandela empfindet sie Bewunderung: »Der ist ein Vorbild, weil er das Land gestaltet hat, ohne Hass zu predigen, obwohl ihm Schlimmes widerfahren ist.« Auch die Obamas bewundert sie.

Ihre engste Beraterin und Heldin ist ihre Mutter, die 20 Jahre im Beruf aussetzte und dann eine berufliche Wiedereingliederung im Bereich Buchhaltung absolvierte. Und noch etwas ringt der Wissenschaftlerin Respekt für die Mutter ab, die auf dem Dorf aufwuchs: Als sie sich für ihren Mann entscheidet, gibt es Familienmitglieder, die die Verbindung mit einem Afrikaner missbilligen. Auch die afrikanische Familie habe wenig Begeisterung für die Wahl der Partnerin durchblicken lassen. Doch die Mutter lässt sich in ihrer Partnerwahl nicht beirren, lernt zur Verständigung mit der Familie des Auserwählten Englisch und setzt ihren Willen durch.

Ihr zwölfjähriges Ich, das nicht weiß, wie es weitermachen soll, würde Addo mit folgenden Worten stärken: »Sei mutig und vertraue dir selbst. Das ist ganz wichtig. Aber man kann sich auch eine zweite Meinung, einen Rat holen.« Und dann kommt wieder so ein Satz, der typisch ist für die Teamplayerin und begeisterte Mentorin: »Man muss nicht immer alles alleine machen.« Es wäre wohl auch selbst für eine Powerfrau wie Addo schwierig, die Welt im Alleingang zu einem besseren Ort zu machen.

you often can't do it all. That's sometimes the most exhausting thing about the job." To compensate, she spends her spare time outside in nature, playing card and board games, and enjoying time with her partner, family and friends. Her sense of humour is also an outlet for relieving tension: "I like to laugh at jokes, well-done comedy and even myself."

If she could do one thing differently, it would be to approach things in a more relaxed way and not to put herself under so much pressure. As a mentor, she also wants to convey that to her protégés. "I tell them, 'Look at what you've already accomplished!'" The virologist also values an open culture that accepts mistakes, which she says exists in the department she runs. "Mistakes are important as long as you learn from them; no one should be afraid of getting something wrong. But that doesn't mean you shouldn't be careful – and you shouldn't make the same mistake twice," says the football fan.

Addo says she grew up with a lot of freedom, yet was very sheltered with her ballet lessons and music tuition. Today, she considers growing up in two cultures a treasure, but as a child she definitely didn't want to stand out: "That was my greatest desire for a long time." Not standing out as Black is a tall order in a mid-sized city with virtually no other Black families in the area. This is also why she sometimes didn't want her father to go to parent-teacher conferences. But even the most sheltered home can't protect a child against racially motivated incidents. On one occasion, dog excrement was smeared onto the family's garage. Another time, her boyfriend was called racist slurs. Addo asserts: "Exclusion can be based on origin, not just skin colour. I feel comfortable in my skin. And my children are growing up in a world that's relatively diverse."

She often visits Ghana, her father's homeland, and has also introduced the culture to her children. Through her work, she's also come to know Botswana, Uganda and South Africa. She has great admiration for South African freedom fighter and former president Nelson Mandela: "He's a role model because he shaped the country without preaching hate, even though bad things happened to him." She also admires the Obamas.

Her hero and closest advisor is her mother, who stopped working for 20 years before completing a re-entry to work programme in the field of accounting. Yet there's also something else that commands the researcher's respect for her mum, who grew up in a small German village: when she decided to marry her husband, there were family members who disapproved of her union with an African man. Likewise, her father's African family had shown little enthusiasm for the pairing. However, Addo's mother was undeterred, learnt English to communicate with her partner's family, and ultimately got her way.

Addo would hearten her twelve-year-old self, who didn't know what direction to take, with these words: "Be brave and trust yourself. That's very important. But you can also get a second opinion or advice." She follows this advice with another tip characteristic of the enthusiastic mentor and team player: "You don't have to do everything alone." Indeed, it would probably be difficult even for a powerful woman like Addo to make the world a better place all by herself.

Enoch Wölfer

IMMOBILIEN- UND INVESTMENTBERATER

»Ich glaube, dass jeder Mensch auf der Erde seine Berufung hat – aber auch die Kraft, Berge zu versetzen. Den ersten Schritt muss er selbst gehen, dann packt das Universum mit an.«

Noch vor wenigen Jahren jonglierte Enoch Wölfer mit dem Fußball, heute mit Geld und Immobilien. »Ich liebe das Risiko und investiere alles, um meine Ziele zu erreichen«, sagt der Jungunternehmer, der mit fünf Brüdern in Duisburg-Hochfeld aufwuchs. Seine Eltern, ghanaische Zuwanderer, schufteten in mehreren Jobs, um ihren Jungen in der neuen Heimat ein gutes Leben zu ermöglichen. »Ich war schon immer Herr über mein eigenes Leben«, erzählt Wölfer, der früh gelernt hat, Verantwortung zu übernehmen und auf sich aufzupassen.

Erste Verkaufserfahrungen sammelt Enoch Wölfer als 14-Jähriger. Mit geliehenem Geld ordert er von einem Großhändler Käppis, die er vor dem Duisburger Hauptbahnhof zum Verkauf anbietet. »Ich habe die Leute einfach angesprochen«, sagt er schmunzelnd. »Das war echte Kaltakquise.« Später handelt er mit Kleidung und gebrauchten Autos. Sein Herz schlägt zu dieser Zeit jedoch für den Fußball, und so setzt er alles daran, Profispieler zu werden und »viel Geld zu verdienen«, so Wölfer. Jede freie Minute verbringt der Jugendliche auf dem Fußballplatz, beim Training, bei Ligaspielen, Turnieren oder in Fußballcamps. Nach dem Abitur wechselt er zu einem niederländischen Verein; der große Traum vom bezahlten Fußball rückt in greifbare Nähe. »Es war eine schöne, aber auch entbehrungsreiche Zeit«, erinnert er sich. Partys und Clubbesuche finden ohne ihn statt. Ausstattung und Fahrten kosten viel Geld, das die Familie nicht hat. Doch dann geht der Club pleite, und Enoch Wölfer wird sich bewusst, dass auch sein Weg hier endet. Er ist 19 Jahre alt, als er die Fußballschuhe an den Nagel hängt.

Den Traum vom großen Geld gibt er nicht auf. Wölfer: »Ich wusste, dass ich niemals normal arbeiten und ein einfaches Angestelltengehalt verdienen wollte.« Über die Jahre ist neben dem Fußball eine neue Leidenschaft gewachsen: Nächtelang hat Enoch Wölfer Bücher über Immobilien gewälzt, sich YouTube-Clips über exklusive Villen in Beverly Hills und Mallorca angeschaut und die Strategien amerikanischer Maklerlegenden studiert. Nach Lionel Messi und Cristiano Ronaldo heißen seine neuen Vorbilder Grant Cardone und Robert Kiyosaki, erfolgreiche Immobilieninvestoren, die sich aus dem Nichts hochgearbeitet haben. Auch der Boxer Muhammad Ali inspiriert den jungen Mann dazu, seine Chancen im Leben zu suchen und wahrzunehmen.

Für einen Crashkurs zum Immobilienmakler leiht Enoch Wölfer sich, wie zuvor schon, Geld von seiner Mutter, die stets an ihn glaubt. Zu Recht: Im Anschluss gründet er in Düsseldorf sein eigenes Unternehmen und vermittelt erst als Partner einer Landesbausparkasse, heute als freier Immobilienmakler Wohnungen und Häuser im Investmentbereich. Vor drei Jahren, so erzählt er, habe er Bilder von seinem Traumauto, einem

REAL ESTATE AND INVESTMENT CONSULTANT

"I believe that everyone on Earth has a calling – and the power to move mountains. You just have to take the first step and then the universe pitches in."

Just a few years ago, Enoch Wölfer was juggling a football. Today, he's juggling money and real estate. "I love risk and invest everything to achieve my goals," says the young entrepreneur, who grew up with five brothers in Duisburg-Hochfeld. His parents, Ghanaian immigrants, toiled at several jobs to give their boys a good life in their new country. "I've always been in charge of my own life," says Wölfer, who learned at an early age to take responsibility and look after himself.

Wölfer gained his first experience in sales at fourteen. Using money he'd borrowed, he ordered baseball caps from a wholesaler and sold them in front of Duisburg's main train station. "I just approached people," he says with a smile. "That was real cold calling." Later, he would trade in clothes and used cars. However, back then his young heart beat for football; Wölfer claims he did everything he could to become a professional player and "earn a lot of money". The youngster spent every free minute on the football pitch, at training, league games, tournaments and football camps. After finishing secondary school, he switched to a Dutch club – and his big dream of paid football was within reach. "It was a good time, but also a time of privation," he remembers. Parties and club visits took place without him. And football equipment and trips cost a lot of money – money his family didn't have. Finally, however, the club went bankrupt… and Wölfer realised that it was the end of the line for him, too. He was nineteen years old when he hung up his football boots for good.

Nevertheless, he hasn't given up on his dream of earning big. Wölfer explains: "I knew that I never wanted to work a normal job and earn a simple white-collar salary." Over the years, a new passion had grown to rival football; the ambitious young man spent his nights poring over books on real estate, watching YouTube clips about exclusive villas in Beverly Hills and Mallorca, and studying the strategies of American real estate legends. After Lionel Messi and Cristiano Ronaldo, his new role models became Grant Cardone and Robert Kiyosaki, successful real estate investors who worked their way up from nothing. The boxer Muhammad Ali also inspires the young man to seek out opportunities in life and grasp them with both hands.

Wölfer once again decided to borrow money – from his mother this time – to complete a crash course in real estate brokerage. His mother's steadfast belief in him was not misplaced; he went on to set up his own company in Düsseldorf, first as a partner of a state building society and later as a freelance real estate agent, brokering apartments and houses in the investment sector. Three years ago, he says,

he hung pictures of his dream car, a Mercedes AMG, and palm tree beaches on his living room wall. Today, the model is in his garage and he's holidaying in Ibiza. According to Wölfer: "Much of what you imagine in life can be manifested through the power of thought." Of course, there were difficult moments, such as when a deal fell through or his overdraft was maxed out, but giving up and accepting employment was unthinkable: "I love my freedom and don't want to spend my life on a hamster wheel." Wölfer agrees that money isn't everything, but makes the point that "it gives me freedoms I didn't have as a kid and allows my family to have a good standard of living". It's nice, he says, to see his parents' joy at his progress – at "how far you can make it as a Black man in Germany". Racism, he says, is something he's rarely experienced. Wölfer also puts that down to his attitude: "The problem is not with me, but with the racist themselves." The businessman sees his skin colour as a sign of strength.

The successful real estate expert can't explain where he draws his strength and energy from, but suggests it may be an earlier near-death experience, when he was rescued from a lake shortly before drowning. Wölfer claims: "On that day, I knew that the good Lord had something great in store for me." As a spiritual man, he's convinced that the soul pursues its destiny while alive. If it fails to fulfil its purpose, it returns after death. This belief is why Wölfer always finds time to pause and be thankful for the most important things in life, despite his fast-paced lifestyle: "I have a roof over my head, I'm healthy, and I have a family. You should never lose sight of those things." He seeks and finds grounding every time he visits Ghana, his parents' homeland.

He would give his twelve-year-old self the following counsel to carry through life: "Be observant so that you can see the opportunities that come your way, no matter how small and unimpressive they might seem to be."

Stephania Mbianda

GYNÄKOLOGIN, AKTIVISTIN UND GESCHÄFTSFRAU

»Ich glaube an die Kraft des Mutes und die Schönheit der Schöpfung, unabhängig von Herkunft, Religion und Hautfarbe.«

Stephania Mbianda ist kein Mensch, der sich einfach so mit Dingen abfindet – weil sie schon immer so waren, weil es opportun wäre oder bequemer. Sie hinterfragt Verhaltensweisen, Traditionen, Klischees und räumt entweder damit auf oder übernimmt sie beziehungsweise festigt sie in ihrem eigenen Leben. Als ihr klar wird, wie widersinnig und unnatürlich es ist, dass sich Schwarze Frauen die Haare glätten, importiert sie Haaröl, damit sie sich leichter bändigen lassen, gründet eine Initiative und das Afro Beauty Festival. »Junge Schwarze Frauen brauchen andere Role Models«, sagt sie als Begründung. Als sie feststellt, dass es nicht ein einziges Kinderbuch über Kamerun gibt, in dem keine Löwen vorkommen, schreibt sie selbst eins, damit ihre Kinder sehen, dass es afrikanisches Leben auch fernab der Safari-Idylle gibt. Und um zu verstehen, warum sie lebt und was Leben bedeutet, entschließt sie sich, Gynäkologin zu werden. Die Liste ließe sich unendlich fortführen. Mbianda lässt sich nicht auf eine Profession oder ein paar wenige Adjektive festlegen. »Ich bin gern Gynäkologin, aber doch nicht nur«, sagt sie.

Als zweites von fünf Kindern kommt Stephania Mbianda im Februar 1985 in Kamerun zur Welt. Ihre Eltern sind beide Lehrer für naturwissenschaftliche Fächer. Sie vermitteln ihren Kindern strenge christliche Werte, behüten sie und schenken ihnen viel Liebe, aber auch Bildung. Der Familie geht es gut in Kamerun, bis Mitte der 1990er-Jahre die Inflationsrate in dem zentralafrikanischen Land auf über 25 Prozent steigt. Das Geld der Familie wird knapp. »Plötzlich hatten wir nur noch ein Auto, mussten ständig zu Fuß gehen. Das war für mich irgendwie ein Knick«, erinnert sich Mbianda. Doch die Familie möchte ohnehin, dass die Kinder in Europa studieren. Sie glauben vor allem an die hervorragende Qualität der Ausbildung in Deutschland. Ihre Tante und ein Bruder leben bereits hier. Also beginnt auch Stephania 2003 ein Medizinstudium in Halle – es ist eine harte Zeit für sie in der ostdeutschen Stadt, eine Zeit, die Mbianda nachhaltig prägt.

Der jungen Frau schlägt offener Rassismus entgegen. »Im Bus hat eine Frau ganz klar gesagt, dass sie sich nicht neben so einen Dreck wie mich setzen wolle«, erinnert sich Mbianda. Sie ist entsetzt, versteht die Welt nicht mehr. Immerhin hatte sie damals 10.000 Euro als Sicherheit mit nach Deutschland bringen müssen – sie will und braucht keine Almosen. Stattdessen lernt sie, dass sie sich als Schwarze Frau immer ein bisschen mehr beweisen muss. Selbstbewusst sei sie schon in ihrer Heimat gewesen, sagt sie, doch in Europa sei diese Eigenschaft auf eine harte Probe gestellt worden. »Wir sind mit Stolz und Menschenwürde aufgewachsen«, erzählt Mbianda. Während ihre Eltern gern im Hintergrund bleiben, drängt sie in die erste Reihe. Es hilft ihr, sich durchzusetzen, als Frau und als Schwarze in Deutschland. Entmutigen lässt sie sich nicht. »Ich habe eine große Klappe.« Doch lange Zeit gestehen andere Menschen ihr, der Schwarzen Frau, das nicht zu.

GYNAECOLOGIST, ACTIVIST AND BUSINESSWOMAN

"I believe in the power of courage and the beauty of creation, regardless of skin tone, origin or religion."

Stephania Mbianda is not a person who simply accepts the status quo, whether because things have always been that way or simply because they seem more opportune or convenient. She challenges behaviours, traditions, and clichés, and either drops them or adopts and reinforces them in her own life. When she realised how absurd and unnatural it is for Black women to straighten their hair, she imported hair oil to help make it easier to tame kinks and coils, founded an initiative, and launched the Afro Beauty Festival: "Young Black women need new role models," she says, explaining her rationale. Likewise, when she realised that there were no children's books about Cameroon that didn't feature lions, she wrote one herself so her children could see that African life also plays out far from the spectacle of the safari. Finally, to understand the meaning of life and her purpose in it, she decided to become a gynaecologist. Yet this short list of accomplishments barely scratches the surface of the multi-talented Renaissance woman; Mbianda refuses to be pinned down to one profession or just a handful of adjectives: "I love being a gynaecologist, but that's not all I am."

Mbianda was born to two science teachers in Cameroon in February 1985, the second of five children. While her parents taught their children strict Christian values, protected them, and gave them a whole lot of love, they also never neglected their education. The family was doing well in Cameroon until inflation in the Central African country rocketed to over 25% in the mid-90s. Money became tight: "Suddenly, we only had one car and had to walk all the time. That was kind of a turning point for me," recalls Mbianda. Nevertheless, the family still wanted the children to study in Europe – and they believed, above all, in the excellent quality of education in Germany. With an aunt and brother already living there, Mbianda started studying medicine in Halle in East Germany in 2003.

This was a difficult period for her and made a lasting impression on the budding medical expert. The young woman often encountered overt racism: "On the bus, a woman said quite clearly that she didn't want to sit next to filth like me," Mbianda recalls. She was horrified and couldn't make sense of it. After all, she'd had to bring €10,000 with her to Germany as a security; she didn't want or need handouts. Instead, she quickly learnt that, as a Black woman, she would always have to prove herself that bit more in her new home. She remembers being very self-confident in her home country, but claims this personality trait was severely tested in Europe: "We grew up with pride and human dignity." While her parents prefer to mill about in the background, Mbianda always wants to position herself front and centre, which helps her to assert herself in Germany as a woman of African heritage. She never lets herself feel

Früh entscheidet sie sich für die Gynäkologie. Es hat etwas mit ihrer Lebensfreude zu tun, mit ihrem Wunsch, das Leben zu verstehen, es schöner und lebenswerter zu machen. »Ich bin gern Geburtshelferin, aber ich stehe auch sehr gern im OP«, sagt sie. Und nicht nur das. Als sie noch während ihres Studiums schwanger wird und 2009 ihren ersten Sohn zur Welt bringt, wird sie plötzlich zur Eventmanagerin und Aktivistin. »Wie alle Schwarzen Frauen habe ich mir damals die Haare geglättet, doch nach meiner Schwangerschaft waren sie plötzlich ganz kaputt«, erinnert sie sich und spricht dann von einer Art »Erleuchtung«. »Mir wurde klar, dass die Natur gut zu allen Menschen ist, wir unser Haar kraus tragen können und es schön ist.« Die Schwarzen Frauen hätten nur verlernt, es richtig zu pflegen – schon in Afrika durch die Kolonisation und noch mehr in Europa. Also beginnt Mbianda, Haarpflegeöl aus Afrika zu importieren und sich auf Facebook mit anderen Frauen auszutauschen. Sie ruft das Afro Beauty Festival ins Leben. Ihre Mission: jungen Schwarzen Frauen zeigen, dass sie schön sind, so wie sie sind.

discouraged: "I have a big mouth." However, for a long time, other people haven't allowed her to embrace this trait as a Black woman.

She decided to go into gynaecology at an early age; it speaks to her zest for life, and her desire to understand it and make it more beautiful and worth living. "I love being an obstetrician, but I also love being in the operating theatre," she says. And that's not all. When she fell pregnant in medical school and gave birth to her first son in 2009, she suddenly became an event manager and activist. "Like all Black women, I straightened my hair at the time, but after my pregnancy my hair was in a sorry state," she recalls. Fortunately, she then had an epiphany: "I realised that nature suits everyone; we can wear our hair curly and it's beautiful." Black women had simply forgotten how to care for it properly – both in Africa due to colonisation and in Europe , where the problem was even worse.. Mbianda therefore started importing hair oil from Africa and exchanging ideas with

Ihr Motor ist dabei der Drang, Dinge zu bewegen und anderen zu helfen. Ihr großes Vorbild ist ihre Mutter. Diese hatte ihre eigene Mutter schon mit 18 verloren und kümmerte sich um ihre drei Schwestern, mit denen Mbianda wie mit Geschwistern aufwuchs. »Meine Mama ist wie ein Esel, sie trägt die Lasten für alle, kümmert sich um andere Frauen und hat selbst eine Initiative gegründet.« Als Mädchen und junge Frau habe sie sich dadurch hin und wieder zurückgesetzt gefühlt. Heute verstehe sie ihre Mutter, auch wenn sie selbst einiges anders mache. Denn Stephania Mbianda ist eine Frau, die zwar Traditionen und Werten verhaftet ist, ihnen aber nicht blind folgt: Morgens um 5:30 Uhr für das Gebet aufzustehen, wie sie es einst als Kind tat, das mache sie heute nicht mehr. Den Rat, den ihre Mutter ihr mit auf den Weg gab, habe sie verinnerlicht: Auch als Frau darf man sich entscheiden, ob man eine Familie haben will oder ob man lieber beruflich Karriere macht und sich auf verschiedenen Ebenen in die Gesellschaft einbringt.

Mbianda gelingt dies alles, und das mit einer Kraft, die kaum vorstellbar ist. Schon im Studium lernt sie ihren heutigen Mann kennen und bekommt drei Kinder mit ihm. »Ohne ihn hätte ich das alles nicht geschafft und würde es auch heute nicht schaffen«, sagt sie. Als ihr Mann einen Job in Frankreich angeboten bekommt, lebt sie dort mit ihm und fährt mehrmals die Woche in die Klinik nach Saarbrücken. »Damals bin ich vier Stunden zur Arbeit gependelt«, erzählt sie. Inzwischen lebt die Familie wieder überwiegend in Deutschland. Manchmal wundere sie sich selbst über ihre Energie und ihren Mut, etwa schon mit 23 Jahren zu heiraten, als Studentin ein Kind zu bekommen und in Bayern, wo sie einige Zeit lebte, für die CSU zu kandidieren. Zugleich weiß sie: »Ich bin ein Mensch, der begeistern und andere mitreißen kann.« Das gebe ihr Kraft. Und sie brauche den Austausch mit anderen Menschen. »Durch andere entdeckt man sich selbst«, ist sie überzeugt. Ihr Lachen helfe ihr dabei. »Eine Kollegin hat einmal zu mir gesagt: ›Du bist wie eine Sonne, die Wärme gibt und strahlt.‹« Seitdem wisse sie ihr Lachen als Geschenk zu schätzen. Dankbar sei sie für die große Kraft, die sie habe: für ihre Kinder, für ihren Mann, ihre Eltern und auch für die Möglichkeiten, die ihr Deutschland biete.

Mit ihrer Hautfarbe hat sie längst Frieden geschlossen, auch wenn sie sich darauf ebenso wenig reduzieren lassen will wie auf ihren Hauptberuf. »Meine Hautfarbe ist ein wichtiger Teil meiner Identität, meine Begleiterin. Ich trage sie mit Stolz.« Das sei ihr wichtig, damit sie es ihren Kindern weitergeben könne. Nur so könnten auch sie Rassismus begegnen. »Rassismus ist dumm, unmenschlich und unfair, vor allem ist er ein Zeichen von Unsicherheit«, ist sie überzeugt. Sie wünscht sich Toleranz und Nachsicht, denn sie weiß: »Manchmal verletzt man andere auch aus Unsicherheit.« Früher habe sie häufig mit Wut und Schroffheit reagiert, im Laufe der Jahre aber gelernt, an sich selbst zu arbeiten.

Ihrem zwölfjährigen Ich würde sie raten, auf den eigenen Instinkt zu vertrauen, sein eigenes Ding zu machen. »Ich habe viel gekämpft«, sagt sie – für sich und so auch für ihre Kinder, für Schwarze Frauen und für die Gesellschaft. Stephania Mbianda ist eine ungewöhnliche Frau: konservativ und weltoffen, traditionell und progressiv. »Ich glaube, ich bin ein seltsamer Mix«, sagt sie über sich und lacht dieses Lachen, das den Raum erstrahlen lässt und die Herzen der Menschen öffnet.

other women on Facebook. Then, she launched the Afro Beauty Festival. Her mission? To show young Black women that they're beautiful just the way they are.

In all this, her driving force was the urge to help others and inspire change. Her greatest role model is her mother. The woman had already lost her own mother at the age of eighteen and subsequently raised her three sisters – meaning Mbianda grew up with them as if they were siblings: "My mum is like a donkey; she carries everyone's burdens, looks after other women, and even founded an initiative herself." As a girl and young woman, she sometimes felt sidelined. Today, she understands her mother, even if she chooses to do some things differently. Indeed, Mbianda may be attached to traditions and values, but she's a woman who doesn't follow them blindly. She no longer gets up at 5.30am to pray as she did as a child, for instance. She's taken her mother's advice to heart: "Even as a woman, you can decide whether you want to have a family or whether you'd prefer to pursue a career and contribute to society in a different way."

Boasting an unimaginable strength, Mbianda has managed to have it all. She met her current husband while still at university and had three children with him: "I wouldn't have achieved any of this and I wouldn't be able to juggle it all today without him." When her husband was offered a job in France, she moved there with him and commuted to a German clinic in Saarbrücken several days a week. "Back then, I commuted four hours a day," she recounts. Nowadays, the family lives mostly in Germany again. Sometimes she's astonished by her energy and courage, having married at the age of 23, had her first child as a student, and then run for the conservative Christian Social Union (CSU) in Bavaria, where she lived for a time. At the same time, she knows: "I'm a person who can inspire others to follow my lead." This gives her strength. She also acknowledges a need to dialogue with other people and strongly believes that "you can only discover yourself through the eyes of others". Her laugh helps her in this endeavour: "A colleague once told me: 'You're like a sun that beams warmth and light'." Since then, she's appreciated her laughter as a gift. She's grateful for her incredible strength, for her children, husband, and parents, and for the opportunities offered to her in Germany.

Mbianda has long made peace with her skin colour, although she no more wishes to be reduced to it than to her profession: "My skin colour is an important part of my identity and will always be with me. I wear it with pride." This is important to her and she's eager to pass this self-acceptance on to her children. To her, this is the only way that they, too, will be able to confront racism: "Racism is stupid, inhumane and unfair. Above all, it's a sign of insecurity," she says with conviction. She wishes for tolerance and forbearance because she knows that "sometimes you can hurt others out of insecurity". In the past, she often reacted with anger and abrasiveness, but over the years she's learnt to work on herself.

She would tell her twelve-year-old self to trust her instincts and do her own thing. "I've fought a lot," she says – for herself, as well as for her children, for Black women, and for society. Mbianda is a woman of contradictions: conservative yet cosmopolitan, and traditional yet progressive. "I think I'm an unusual mix," she observes with a laugh that lights up the room and opens people's hearts.

Paguiel Mlapa

BANKDIREKTOR

»Ich glaube an die Kraft des eisernen Willens, um seine Ziele zu erreichen – auch wenn man hin und wieder mal einen falschen Abzweig nimmt.«

Wenn Paguiel Mlapa das Haus verlässt, kann es schon mal vorkommen, dass er an der Eingangstür umdreht, um die Schuhe im Flur ordentlich nebeneinander aufzustellen. »Ich bin so deutsch«, sagt er dann über sich und lacht. Von seinen Eltern hat er das nicht, seine Frau Manda treibt er damit in den Wahnsinn, doch sie weiß ihn zu nehmen, und sein kleiner Sohn hat diesen Ordnungssinn längst von ihm übernommen. Es ist nicht das Einzige, was Mlapa an sich als typisch deutsch bezeichnet. Er trägt auch gern bayerische Tracht, liebt die strukturierten Abläufe in seiner Bank, hat gerade mit seiner Familie das Wandern in den Voralpen für sich entdeckt, spricht mit bayerischem Akzent – und stammt aus Lomé, der Hauptstadt von Togo.

»Mein Vater ist früh nach Deutschland gekommen, um hier sein Glück zu suchen«, erzählt der 1988 geborene Mlapa. Seine Familie lässt der Vater zunächst in dem westafrikanischen Land zurück – und ist ihr doch immer ganz nah. »Er hat uns keine Briefe geschrieben, sondern Kassetten besprochen, damit wir seine Stimme hören konnten«, erinnert sich Mlapa. Mitte der 1990er-Jahre holt der Vater seine Familie nach, in eine Flüchtlingsunterkunft in München. Die vierköpfige Familie lebt auf 25 Quadratmetern. In dem Stockbett schlafen die Eltern oben, die beiden Brüder unten. »Mit Schnüren haben wir Linien gezogen, um das Schlafzimmer von unserem Ess- und Wohnzimmer abzutrennen«, sagt Mlapa. Es ist beengt, doch den kleinen Paguiel stört das kaum. Er wird direkt in die zweite Klasse eingeschult, ohne ein Wort Deutsch zu sprechen. Nach sechs Monaten beherrscht er die Sprache perfekt. »Ich bin in der Klasse wahnsinnig gut aufgenommen und immer überall eingeladen worden«, erzählt er.

Paguiel Mlapa besucht die Realschule und macht anschließend das Fachabitur. So recht weiß er nicht, welchen Beruf er ergreifen soll. Marketing interessiert ihn. Doch dann schwärmt eine Nachbarin von ihrem Job bei der Münchner Bank. Die Familie Mlapa wohnt da längst in einer kleinen Wohnung in München-Unterföhring. Insgesamt zwölf Bewerbungen schreibt der Abiturient, zwei davon an Banken. Beide bieten ihm eine Ausbildung an, er entscheidet sich für die Münchner Bank. »Da hatte ich gleich das Gefühl, dass das gut passt«, sagt er. Er behält recht: Zunächst arbeitet er als Kundenberater und steigt dann ins Privatkundengeschäft auf. 2017 übernimmt er die Filialleitung in München-Haidhausen und im November 2021 beruft ihn die Bank zum Filialdirektor.

Geld und Gesundheit sind zwei Dinge, die dem freundlichen und extrem fokussierten Bankkaufmann wichtig sind. »Geld gibt Sicherheit und nimmt einem viele Sorgen, die Gesundheit braucht man, um das Leben genießen zu können«, begründet Mlapa seine Einstellung und fügt hinzu, dass Familie und Liebe natürlich auch dazugehören. Seine Frau, die selbst afrikanische und dazu deutsche Wurzeln hat, halte ihm den Rücken frei.

BANK DIRECTOR

"I believe in the strength of an iron will to help you achieve your goals – even if you take a wrong turn here or there."

When Paguiel Mlapa leaves the house, he sometimes turns around at his front door to line up the shoes in the hallway in a neat row. "I'm so German," he laughs. He didn't get that from his parents and it drives his wife Manda crazy, but she's used to it – and his little son has long since inherited his sense of order. Yet this isn't the only thing about Mlapa that he'd describe as typically German. He also likes to wear traditional Bavarian clothing, loves the structured processes at his bank, has just discovered hiking in the foothills of the Alps with his family, speaks with a Bavarian accent… and comes from Lomé, the capital of Togo.

"My father came to Germany at an early age to seek his fortune," says Mlapa, who was born in 1988. Initially, his father left his family behind in the West African country, yet he always remained very close to them. "He didn't write us any letters; he sent cassettes so we could hear his voice," recalls Mlapa. In the 90s, Mlapa's father brought his family of four to a refugee shelter in Munich, where they shared a living space measuring just 25 sqm. The parents slept on the top bunk bed and the two brothers slept on the bottom one. "We drew lines with shoe laces to separate the bedroom from our living/dining room," recalls Mlapa. It was cramped, but that didn't bother little Paguiel. He soon started school and was placed directly into year two without speaking a word of German. After six months, he'd mastered the language perfectly. "I was incredibly well received in the class and was always invited everywhere," he shares.

Mlapa moved up to secondary school and then completed a vocational school-leaving qualification. He wasn't really sure what career to pursue. Marketing appealed to him, but then a neighbour gushed to him about her job at the Münchner Bank credit union. By then, the Mlapa family had been living in a small flat in Munich-Unterföhring for some time. The school leaver sent out twelve different applications, including two to banks. When both offered him an apprenticeship, he chose Münchner Bank. "I instantly got the feeling that it would be a good fit," he says. He was right. He first worked as a customer advisor, before being promoted to private customer business. In 2017, he took over as Branch Manager in Munich-Haidhausen and, in November 2021, he was made Branch Director.

Money and health are two things that are very important to the friendly and focused banker. "Money gives you security and takes away a lot of worries, and you need your health to be able to enjoy life," says Mlapa, explaining his attitude, adding that love and family are of course part and parcel of this too; his wife, who has Afro-German roots herself, always has his back. Although he and his parents began their lives in Germany with little money to speak of, he

Auch wenn er mit seinen Eltern mit nur wenig Geld in Deutschland gestartet sei – gefehlt habe es ihm und seinem jüngeren Bruder, dem Profifußballer Peniel, nie an etwas. Das verdanke er seinen Eltern, seinen großen Vorbildern. Drei Jobs machte sein Vater über viele Jahre: Morgens trug er Zeitungen aus, dann schob er Schichten in einer Fabrik und abends ging er putzen. Mlapas Mutter arbeitete als Küchenhilfe und ging ebenfalls putzen. »Diese Arbeitsmoral hat mich tief beeindruckt und sehr geprägt«, sagt Mlapa. Sein Vater habe ihm zudem einen wichtigen Leitsatz mit auf den Lebensweg gegeben: »Es gibt keine Arbeit, die leicht ist. Deswegen verdient auch jede Arbeit Respekt.« Dabei sei es egal, ob man Putzmann, Bundesligafußballer oder Bankdirektor sei. Diese Einstellung habe er verinnerlicht.

Seine eigene Berufswahl hat er nie bereut oder infrage gestellt. Das liege wohl auch an seinen vielen Eigenschaften, die ihn dafür prädestinieren würden: Mlapa beschreibt sich selbst als nicht nur extrem fokussiert, er handele auch überlegt, gehe immer einen Schritt nach dem nächsten. Noch dazu sei er Teamplayer und Teamleiter zugleich. »Ich gebe alles für meine Mitarbeiter, und das wissen sie auch«, sagt er. Mlapa bringt das mit, was auf Neudeutsch als »Emotional Banking« bezeichnet wird. Er verbindet Sachlichkeit mit Herzenswärme.

Seine Hautfarbe sieht er dabei vor allem als Ansporn, denn noch immer ist die Finanzwelt weiß. »Der Vorteil ist: Ich falle immer und überall auf. Die Menschen erinnern sich an mich«, sagt er. Zugleich aber würden sie auch doppelt so gut zuhören, manchmal aus Argwohn, manchmal aus Bewunderung. »Ich thematisiere das nicht, auch weil Hautfarbe manchmal als Ausrede genutzt wird.« Die Mlapas haben Schwarze und weiße Freunde. Hautfarbe ist für sie kein Thema.

Mlapa ist selbstbewusst – das strahlt er aus, das verschaffe ihm Respekt und Ansehen. Und er kann sich anpassen, fühlt sich in jeder Gesellschaft wohl, wie er sagt. Er nenne sich daher gern mal »das Chamäleon«. »Ich komme mit den Menschen auf wichtigen Finanztreffen ebenso gut klar wie mit jedem an der Supermarktkasse.« Als Gründe dafür nennt er seine Offenheit, sein Interesse und dass er die Menschen so sein lasse, wie sie sind, vorausgesetzt, sie würden niemandem schaden.

Stolz ist der Bankdirektor auf seinen 2014 geborenen Sohn. »Der ist hübsch, intelligent, bringt mich mit seiner kindlichen Ernsthaftigkeit zum Lachen und macht mich glücklich, auch weil er so stolz auf mich ist.« Er sei dankbar dafür, so Mlapa, dass er in Deutschland lebe. »Aber ich hätte auch etwas in Togo erreicht, hätte meine Eltern nicht enttäuscht, aber hier in Deutschland gibt es mehr Möglichkeiten.« Denn, so sagt der gläubige Katholik: »Wenn ich etwas anfange, dann schaffe ich das auch. Das ist eine Gabe, die mir Gott geschenkt hat.« Eine von vielen. Zugleich hat Mlapa einen Rat für sein zwölfjähriges Ich und alle anderen Kinder und Jugendlichen: »Selbst wenn du mal die falsche Abfahrt genommen hast, kannst du immer noch dein Ziel erreichen.«

An die Heimat seiner Vergangenheit hat er kaum noch Erinnerungen, auch wenn er seine Tanten und Onkel, Cousinen und Cousins immer mal wieder besucht. Seine Eltern möchten eines Tages wieder zurück nach Togo, doch für Mlapa ist München längst zur Heimat geworden. »Hier bin ich gewachsen.« Mlapa und seine Familie haben ihren Platz gefunden, ganz selbstverständlich als Schwarze im noch immer überwiegend weißen Deutschland, im weißen Bayern und in der weißen Finanzwelt. Es ist für sie eine Selbstverständlichkeit.

and his younger brother, professional footballer Peniel, have never wanted for anything. He owes that to his parents, who are his greatest role models. For many years, his father worked three jobs: in the morning, he delivered newspapers, then he worked shifts in a factory, and in the evenings he cleaned. Mlapa's mother was a kitchen hand and also cleaned. "This work ethic made a strong impression on me and shaped who I am today," says Mlapa. His father also taught him an important guiding principle: "There's no work that's easy, which is why every job demands respect." It doesn't matter whether you're a cleaner, a Bundesliga footballer or a bank director. And Mlapa took this attitude to heart.

He's never doubted or regretted his own choice of profession, probably due to the many qualities that make him seem born for the job; Mlapa not only describes himself as extremely focused, but also as very deliberate, always proceeding one step at a time. In addition, he's both a team player and a team leader. "I give everything for my staff and they know that," he explains. Mlapa brings a new concept to the table called "emotional banking", combining objectivity with genuine warmth.

He explains that while the financial world is still very white, his skin colour emboldens him to do this. "The advantage is that I always stand out everywhere. People remember me," he states. At the same time, they listen to him twice as carefully, sometimes out of suspicion, sometimes out of admiration: "I don't make anything of it, also because skin colour is sometimes used as an excuse." The Mlapas have Black and white friends, and skin colour isn't an issue for them.

Mlapa is self-assured – and the confidence he exudes is what earns him respect and recognition. He considers himself very adaptable and feels at ease in any company. For this reason, he likes to call himself 'the chameleon': "I get along just as well with businesspeople at important financial meetings as with cashiers at the supermarket." By way of explanation, he cites his open-mindedness, his genuine interest in others, and the fact that he lets people be themselves as long as they aren't hurting anyone.

The bank director is proud of his son, born in 2014: "He's handsome, intelligent, makes me laugh with his childlike earnestness, and makes me happy because he's so proud of me." Mlapa is also grateful that he lives in Germany: "I would have made something of myself in Togo, too; I wouldn't have disappointed my parents. But there are more opportunities here in Germany." Indeed, the devout Catholic asserts that "if I start something, I'll finish it. That's my gift from God." One of many, it would seem. Equally, Mlapa would offer his twelve-year-old self the same advice that he'd offer to all other children and young people: "Even if you've taken a wrong turn, you can still reach your destination."

He has hardly any childhood memories of his distant homeland, even though he visits his aunts, uncles and cousins from time to time. His parents would like to return to Togo one day, but Munich has long since become home for Mlapa: "I grew up here." The banker and his family have found their place as Black Germans in a predominantly white country, in white Bavaria, and in the white world of finance. To them, it comes quite naturally.

Adelaide Wolters

UNTERNEHMERIN

»Ich glaube daran, dass es unsere Aufgabe ist, einander als gleichwertig zu erkennen mit den Augen von Gott, denn der hat uns alle gleichwertig geschaffen.«

Die Küche in der elterlichen Wohnung ist oft blockiert. Dort hantiert die Teenagerin Adelaide mit einem Mixer und kombiniert die verschiedenen Inhaltsstoffe für ihre Cremes immer wieder neu. Das junge Mädchen hat sich in den Kopf gesetzt, die Lösung für ihr größtes Problem zu finden, das ihr seit der Grundschulzeit immer wieder Hänseleien eingebracht hat: Ihre Haut ist stark pigmentiert und unrein. Infolgedessen ist ihr Selbstbewusstsein am Nullpunkt. Die von ihr zuvor konsultierten Hautärzte waren ratlos gewesen und hatten ihr zu verstehen gegeben: Das komme eben bei Schwarzen Menschen vor, damit müsse sie leben. Es ist ihre Mutter, die ihr wieder Mut macht, indem sie ihrer unglücklichen Tochter sagt, dass sich auch Ärzte irren könnten und sie doch mal im Internet zu ihren Hautproblemen recherchieren solle. Das tut sie und mixt fleißig weiter. Vier Jahre dauert es, dann hat Adelaide eine Creme kreiert, die ihre Haut glättet und die Hyperpigmentierungen reduziert. Familie, Freunde und Bekannte probieren die Creme ebenfalls aus und sind begeistert von der Wirkung. Mit 22 Jahren, nach ihrem Abitur und einer um ein Jahr verkürzten Ausbildung zur Hotelfachfrau, gründet die Hamburgerin ihre Kosmetikfirma Unrefined Riches.

Anfangs macht sie alles selbst und hat daneben noch mehrere Jobs, um über die Runden zu kommen. So arbeitet sie etwa am Empfang und in der Buchhaltung, um ihren Lebensunterhalt zu bestreiten. Doch seit 2020 wächst das Geschäft. Die Tochter eines Kochs und einer Reinigungskraft aus Ghana stellt 2021 erstmals Mitarbeiter ein, zumal sie selbst parallel zur Konsolidierung der Firma Betriebswirtschaftslehre und Wirtschaftspsychologie studiert. Doch die Firma geht für sie klar vor. Adelaide lässt sich für zwei Semester beurlauben, um sich ganz der Entwicklung ihres Start-ups zu widmen, dessen Anfänge holprig verlaufen: »Ich habe sehr viele Fehler gemacht, die auch zu Fehlinvestitionen geführt haben. Zum Beispiel habe ich mir vor einer Großbestellung keine Muster von den Verpackungen besorgt. Und ich habe mich nicht mit Förderkrediten befasst, als alle meine Kreditanfragen abgelehnt wurden.« Vonseiten der Banken heißt es, sie sei zu jung und habe noch zu wenig Arbeitserfahrung. Schließlich erhält sie einen Kredit von der Familie. Die hat für sie, die seit 2017 mit Chris Wolters verheiratet ist und mittlerweile mit ihm in einem Dorf bei Paderborn ein Haus bewohnt, einen hohen Stellenwert. Besonders von ihrer Mutter wird sie stark geprägt. »Meine Mutter ist mein Vorbild und meine Heldin. Sie hat mich gelehrt, stark zu sein, beständig zu bleiben und das Ziel nicht aus den Augen zu verlieren.«

Es sind nicht nur theoretische Ratschläge, die ihre Mutter ihr mit auf den Weg gibt, sondern diese lebt ihrer Tochter auch vor, nicht aufzugeben und zu kämpfen, besonders als ein Unheil über die Familie hereinbricht: Adelaide ist zwölf Jahre alt, da wird ihr Vater aus Deutschland abgeschoben. In den folgenden Jahren sind die Kinder viel auf sich allein gestellt, denn die Mutter hat an manchen Tagen drei Beschäftigungen als

ENTREPRENEUR

"I believe in recognising each other as equals through the eyes of God, for He created us all equal."

The kitchen in her parents' apartment was often occupied… because it was there that the teenaged Adelaide spent much of her time tinkering with a mixer to combine the ingredients for her creams. The young girl had set her mind on finding the solution to her biggest problem – one for which she'd been teased since primary school: her skin was blemished and hyperpigmented. As a result, her self-confidence was at rock bottom. The dermatologists she'd consulted were always at a loss and told her it happens to Black people; she'd just have to live with it. It was her mother who reassured her, telling her unhappy daughter that even doctors can be wrong and that she should do some research on the internet about her skin problems. She did this – and carried on mixing away. It would be four years before Adelaide successfully created a cream that smoothed her skin and reduced her hyperpigmentation. Family, friends and acquaintances also tried the cream and were thrilled with the results. After finishing school and completing a one-year apprenticeship as a hotel manager, the Hamburg native founded her cosmetics company Unrefined Riches at the age of 22.

In the beginning, she did everything herself and worked several jobs to make ends meet, taking roles as both a receptionist and bookkeeper. The business finally took off in 2020. In 2021, the daughter of a cook and cleaner from Ghana hired her first employees. She's now studying business administration and business psychology as she consolidates the company. Nevertheless, the company remains her first priority; Adelaide is taking two semesters off to devote herself entirely to the development of her start-up, which had a bumpy start in life: "I made a lot of mistakes, which also led to bad investments. For example, I didn't get samples of the packaging before placing a large order, and I didn't look into development loans when all my loan requests were rejected." According to the banks, she's too young and has too little work experience. In the end, she secured a loan from her family – and family has always been of great importance to the entrepreneur, who married Chris Wolters in 2017 and now lives with him in a village near Paderborn. She's strongly influenced by her mother: "My mum is my role model and my hero. She's taught me to be strong and consistent, and to never lose sight of my goals".

But her mother doesn't just offer theoretical advice; she also models for her daughter not to give up and to keep fighting, especially when disaster strikes the family. Adelaide was just twelve years old when her father was deported from Germany. In the years that followed, the children were often left to their own devices, as their mother had to work three jobs as a cleaner on some days. "She tried to hide her financial difficulties from us and managed to help us to do a lot,"

Reinigungskraft. »Sie hat versucht, ihre finanziellen Schwierigkeiten vor uns zu verbergen, und es geschafft, uns vieles zu ermöglichen«, so Wolters. Kurz vor ihrem Abitur kann der Vater dann wieder aus Ghana zu seiner Familie zurückkehren.

Wurzeln in Ghana zu haben, mache sie stolz, sagt Adelaide Wolters. »Mein Opa war im Distrikt Bosomtwe in Kuntanase König. Auch meine Hautfarbe ist nichts, wofür ich mich schämen müsste. Sie ist ein Teil von mir, der zu mir passt.« In den ersten beiden Schuljahren verunsichern sie jedoch die Fragen ihrer Mitschülerinnen und Mitschüler, warum ihre Haare und ihre Haut so aussehen würden. Die Unternehmerin: »Ich habe mir gewünscht, einmal einzuschlafen, und am nächsten Tag wache ich auf und bin weiß und angepasst.«

Heute sei sie dankbar dafür, was ihre Eltern ihr alles mitgegeben hätten, und meint damit unter anderem, dass sie aus Negativem etwas Positives geschaffen habe. Sie hat sich dafür entschieden, Produkte für alle Hauttypen, nicht nur für Schwarze Menschen, zu produzieren. »Ich kenne ja das Gefühl, ausgeschlossen zu werden, und wollte nicht in die Fußstapfen von den Menschen treten, die mich ausgeschlossen hatten.« Ihr Antrieb sei es, die Kosmetikbranche aufzumischen, die Standards neu zu setzen. »Jede und jeder sollte sich in seiner Haut wohlfühlen können.« Ihre Herkunft mache sie stolz, weil die Ghanaer für ihre Unabhängigkeit gekämpft hätten. Ghana habe einer Studie zufolge außerdem die meisten Schwarzen Gründerinnen in Afrika. Die Heimat ihrer Eltern ist ihr sehr vertraut: Bis zur Abschiebung des Vaters war die Familie, zu der auch ein Bruder und zwei Schwestern gehörten, einmal im Jahr nach Ghana geflogen.

»Ich hätte meinem zwölfjährigen Ich geraten, meine Eltern zu fragen, woher wir kommen und mir etwas über die Geschichte Ghanas zu erzählen. Dann hätte ich als Kind einen anderen Blick auf mich selbst gehabt.« Jetzt, als Erwachsene, ändert sich ihr Blickwinkel durch das Lesen von Büchern zum Thema Persönlichkeitsentwicklung und durch das Studium der Bibel. »Da findet man etwas zu jedem Lebensabschnitt«, ist ihre Erfahrung. Rassismus bedeutet für Wolters, einer Ideologie anzuhängen, die davon ausgehe, dass eine Gruppe von Menschen mehr Wert habe als eine andere. Und dass ein System etabliert werde, das eine Gruppe unterdrücke und einer anderen zum Vorteil gereiche. Das könne beispielsweise in der Sprache oder im Schulsystem zum Ausdruck kommen.

Wolters setzt auf starkes Wachstum ihrer Firma, doch hat sie aus ihren Fehlern gelernt, geduldiger zu sein: »Dadurch habe ich gemerkt, dass ich keine übereilten Entscheidungen treffen, sondern lieber noch mal eine Nacht darüber schlafen sollte. Eine Existenzgründung ist ein Marathon, kein Sprint. Manchmal überrascht mich mein Durchhaltevermögen. Es gab Situationen während der Gründung – bei anderen Dingen hätte ich da schon aufgegeben.« Ihre Fehler bringen sie aber auch zum Lachen: »Wenn ich an etwas nicht gedacht habe, sage ich zu mir selbst: Das hättest du jetzt aber wissen müssen.« Trotz Expansionskurs sind der Unternehmerin bestimmte Werte wichtig. »Ich mache das nicht nur, um Geld zu verdienen. Meine Kunden motivieren mich.«

Einer ihrer größten Wünsche aber lässt sich nur mit einem größeren Vermögen verwirklichen. »Ich träume davon, dass ich eines Tages nach Hamburg zu meinen Eltern fahren und ihnen sagen kann, dass sie genug gearbeitet haben und ihre Jobs kündigen können. Sie haben mich immer unterstützt, deshalb möchte ich ihnen etwas zurückgeben.« Dann wären die Eltern sicher endgültig davon überzeugt, dass die von ihnen anfangs mit Skepsis betrachtete Entscheidung ihrer Tochter richtig war, statt eines sicheren Angestelltenverhältnisses im Hotelgewerbe das Risiko der Selbstständigkeit auf sich zu nehmen. Immerhin waren sie ganz nah dabei, als diese ihren Anfang nahm, damals in ihrer Küche.

Wolters said. Shortly before they finished school, their father was able to return from Ghana to be with his family.

Wolters is proud of her Ghanaian roots: "My grandfather was king of the Bosomtwe district of Kuntanase. And my skin colour isn't something I'm ashamed of. It's part of me and it suits me." However, during her first two years at school, she was unsettled by her classmates asking why her hair and skin look the way they do. The entrepreneur explains: "I once wished I could go to sleep and wake up the next morning to find that I was white and fitted in."

Today, she's grateful for everything her parents have given her and believes that she's turned a negative into a positive. She's chosen to make products for all skin types, not just Black people: "After all, I know the feeling of being excluded and I didn't want to follow in the footsteps of the people who'd excluded me." She's driven by a desire to shake up the beauty industry and set new standards: "Anyone and everyone should be able to feel comfortable in their own skin." Wolters is proud of her heritage because Ghanaians fought for their independence. What's more, studies show that Ghana boasts the highest number of Black female founders in Africa. Her parents' homeland is very familiar to her; until her father was deported, she flew to Ghana with her parents, brother and two sisters once a year.

"I would tell my twelve-year-old self to ask my parents where we come from and to ask about the history of Ghana – then I would have had a different view of myself as a child." Now, as an adult, her perspective is changing thanks to reading books on personal development and studying the Bible. In her experience, "the Bible has something to offer at every stage of life." For Wolters, racism means adhering to an ideology which assumes that one group of people has more value than another, causing a system to be established that oppresses one group for the benefit of another – and that this can ultimately be reflected in language or in the school system, for instance.

Wolters is predicting strong growth for her company, but her past mistakes have taught her to be more patient: "I've come to realise that I shouldn't make hasty decisions; it's better to sleep on it. Starting a business is a marathon, not a sprint. Sometimes my stamina surprises me; there were situations during the start-up phase where I'd have given up with something else by then." Yet her mistakes also make her laugh: "When I haven't thought of something, I say to myself: you really should know that by now!" Despite her company's growth, certain values remain important to the entrepreneur: "I don't do this just to make money – I'm motivated by my customers."

Nevertheless, one of her dearest wishes can only come true off the back of a larger fortune: "I have a dream that one day I'll go to Hamburg to visit my parents and tell them that they've worked enough and can quit their jobs. They've always supported me, so I want to give them something in return." Then her parents would surely be convinced once and for all that their daughter's decision to embrace the risks of self-employment instead of pursuing a secure, salaried position in the hotel industry – a decision they initially viewed with scepticism – was the right one. After all, they were right there when it all began years ago in their kitchen.

Saliya Kahawatte

UNTERNEHMER

»Ich glaube an mich selbst – das hat mich das Leben gelehrt.«

Sein Leben wurde anhand seiner Autobiografie verfilmt. Es ist eine Geschichte, wie kein Drehbuchautor sie sich jemals hätte ausdenken können. Die Lebensgeschichte eines Mannes, der mit unüberwindlich erscheinenden Hindernissen und Niederlagen zu kämpfen hatte und diese mit Willenskraft, Disziplin, Ehrgeiz und Unterstützung zahlreicher Menschen gemeistert hat. »Je tiefer ich gefallen bin, desto stärker hat es mich gemacht«, sagt Saliya Kahawatte im Rückblick auf sein bisheriges Leben. Dieses beginnt 1969 in Freiberg in Sachsen. Die Eltern sind beide Akademiker. Seine Mutter ist Deutsche, sein Vater, ein promovierter Physiker, stammt aus Sri Lanka und ist als Austauschstudent in die sächsische Kleinstadt gekommen. Als Saliya vier Jahre alt ist, fliehen seine Eltern mit ihm und seiner 15 Monate jüngeren Schwester aus der DDR. Die Geschwister wachsen in einem Dorf bei Osnabrück auf, wo die Eltern als Internatslehrer arbeiten. Die drei Schwarzen Familienmitglieder sind die einzigen Ausländer in der Gegend. Die Kinder werden anfangs im Kindergarten gehänselt und haben es schwer, Freunde zu finden. Das ändert sich jedoch bald nach dem Eintritt in den Turnverein und die lokale Pfadfindergruppe. Zu Hause hat Saliya unter seinem herrschsüchtigen Vater zu leiden, der den Sohn immer wieder vor anderen Menschen bloßstellt und ihn sogar hin und wieder schlägt. Andere Werte als Angst und Unterwürfigkeit vermittelt ihm sein Großvater, der aus der DDR ins Haus der Familie übersiedelt, als der Junge elf Jahre alt ist. Der Vater der Mutter hat immer ein offenes Ohr für seinen Enkel und lehrt ihn, Herausforderungen anzunehmen. Kahawatte: »Mein Opa war ein Vorbild für mich. Er hat mir viel Kraft gegeben.« Als Saliya 14 Jahre alt ist, stirbt diese für ihn wichtige Bezugsperson.

Ein Jahr später wird der Teenager hart vom Schicksal getroffen. Der begeisterte Läufer, der mehrmals in der Woche für Wettrennen trainiert, erleidet eine akute Netzhautablösung. Innerhalb kurzer Zeit verliert der 15-Jährige 80 Prozent seines Sehvermögens. »Diese Diagnose schüttelt man nicht einfach so ab wie Kopfschmerzen. Ich dachte: ›Jetzt bist du behindert.‹« Trotz der hochgradigen Sehbehinderung kämpft er darum, das Abitur zu schaffen. Dafür nutzt er die Augen von Schwester, Mutter und einem Nachbarsjungen, die ihm stundenlang Texte vorlesen, und profitiert dabei von seinem guten Gedächtnis. Auch heute noch ist Kahawatte überrascht von seiner damals schon ausgeprägten Akribie und Disziplin, mit der er durchs Leben geht. Das Abi schafft er trotz seiner Behinderung mit einem Notendurchschnitt von drei. Doch ihm ist klar, dass sein Traum, Chirurg zu werden, nicht in Erfüllung gehen kann. Der Berater, den er mit seiner Mutter konsultiert, empfiehlt eine Ausbildung in einer Behinderteneinrichtung oder eines von drei als behindertengerecht geltenden Studienfächern. Doch der Abiturient hat sich als neues Ziel eine Ausbildung in der gehobenen Hotellerie gesetzt, einer internationalen Branche, in der wenigstens seine Hautfarbe nicht von Belang ist. Bei den Bewerbungen verschweigt er sein Handicap – und wird erst zwei Jahrzehnte später mit dem Vorspielen falscher Tatsachen und der damit

ENTREPRENEUR

"Life has taught me to believe in myself."

His life story (as told in his autobiography) has made it to the silver screen – and it's a story that no screenwriter could ever have dreamed up. It tells of a man who's faced seemingly insurmountable odds, and who's overcome them through willpower, discipline, ambition and the support of a great many people. "The further I fell, the stronger it made me," says Saliya Kahawatte, looking back on his life so far. It all began in Freiberg, Saxony, in 1969. Kahawatte's parents were both academics. His mother is German and his father, who boasts a PhD in physics, is Sri Lankan, having first come to the small German town as an exchange student. When Saliya was four years old, he fled East Germany with his parents and his fifteen-month-old sister. The two siblings would grow up in a village near Osnabrück, where their parents worked as boarding school teachers. The three Black family members were the only foreigners in the area. At first, the children were teased in nursery school and had a hard time making friends. However, that soon changed when they joined the gymnastics club and the local scout troop. At home, Saliya suffered at the hands of his domineering father, who repeatedly humiliated his son in front of others and even beat him from time to time. Values other than fear and submissiveness were instilled in the boy by his grandfather, who moved from East Germany to the family home when Kahawatte turned eleven. His mother's father always offered his grandson a listening ear and taught him to face challenges head on. Kahawatte explains: "My grandfather was a role model for me. He gave me great strength." When Kahawatte turned fourteen, this important figure in his life passed away.

Just one year later, the teenager was visited by a terrible misfortune; the enthusiastic runner, who trained several times a week for races, suffered an acute retinal detachment. Shortly thereafter, the fifteen-year-old lost 80% of his vision: "That's not a diagnosis you can just shake off like a headache. I thought to myself: now you're disabled." Despite his profound visual impairment, Kahawatte strived hard to achieve his school-leaving certificate. To do so, he used the eyes of his sister, mother and a young neighbour, who spent hours reading texts to him – a feat made possible thanks to his excellent memory. Even today, Kahawatte is surprised by the meticulous discipline that carries him through life. Despite his disability, he was able to leave school with a GPA of 3.0, equivalent to a grade C. Nevertheless, it was immediately clear to him that he could never achieve his dream of becoming a surgeon. The career advisor he consulted with his mother recommended either an apprenticeship at a facility for the disabled or one of three fields of study considered suitable for those with disabilities. However, the young man instead set himself a new goal: an apprenticeship in the upscale hotel business – leading to an international role in which at least his skin colour would not be an issue. He not only concealed his disability when applying for jobs,

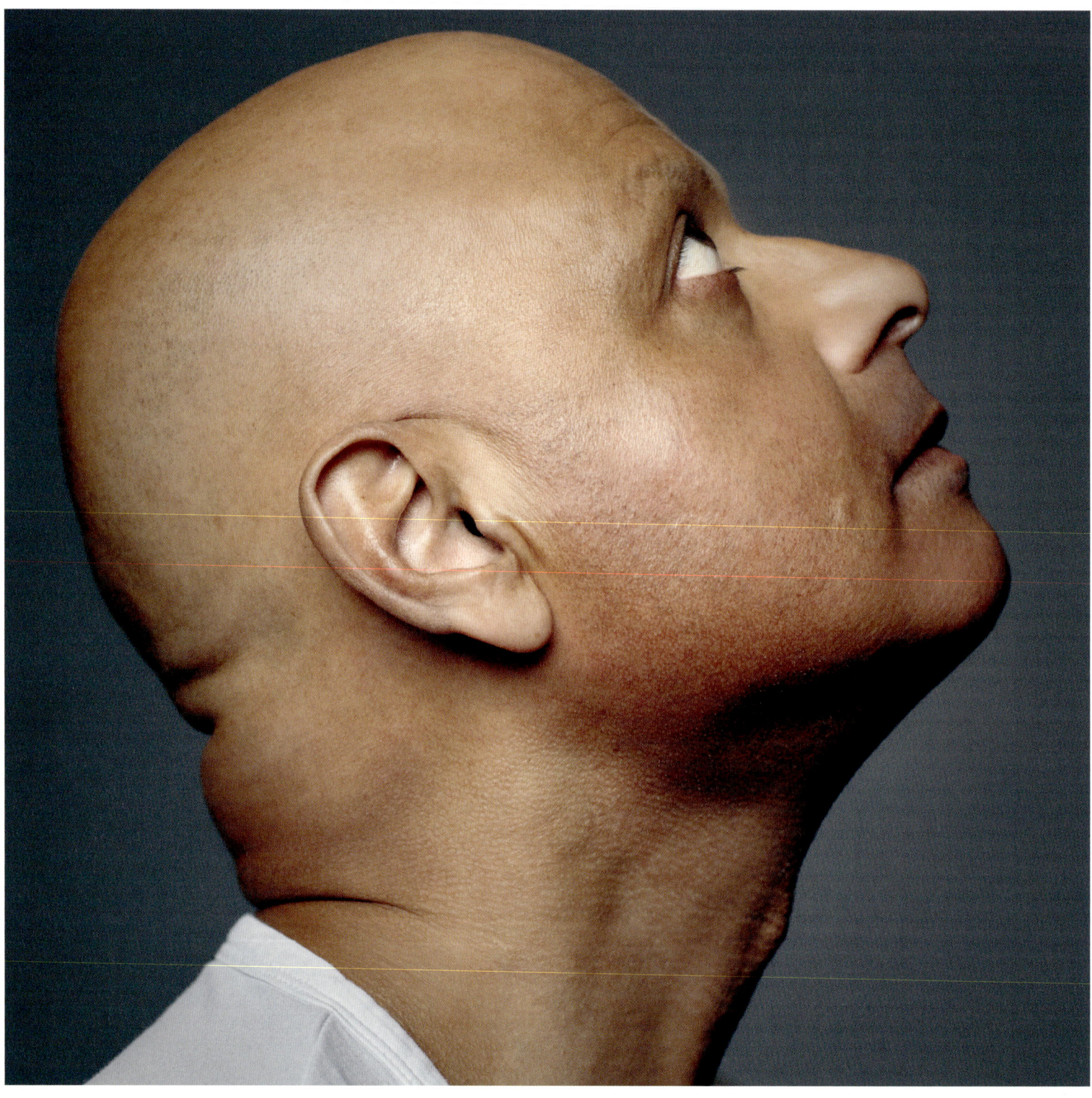

einhergehenden Einbindung von engen Unterstützern wie Freunden, Partnerinnen und Arbeitskollegen aufhören. Dazwischen liegt die Zeit, in der er im Anschluss an seine Ausbildung in Hannover Arbeitserfahrung in der Fünf-Sterne-Hotellerie sammelt und ein erfolgreiches Studium der Hotelbetriebswirtschaftslehre in Hamburg absolviert.

»Ich habe viele Federn lassen müssen«, so Kahawatte. Der Druck im Arbeitsleben, die Angst davor, dass die Lüge auffliegen könnte, ist der Hauptgrund für seinen starken Alkoholkonsum und die Einnahme von Drogen. Am Ende seiner Kräfte angelangt, begeht er einen Suizidversuch. Sein Fazit über diese extreme Phase in seinem Leben: »Ich habe gelernt, die Schuld für Fehler nicht bei anderen zu suchen, sondern erst mal bei mir selbst – und meinen Optimismus nicht zu verlieren.« Diese Einstellung hilft dem Unternehmer, der heute in seiner

but also throughout his employment (with the help of friends, partners and work colleagues), and would only reveal the truth two decades later. During the intervening twenty years, Kahawatte finished his training in Hanover and gained work experience in the five-star hotel industry. He later went on to successfully complete a degree in hotel business administration in Hamburg.

"I took some losses along the way," he admits. The pressures of work and his fear of being caught lying about his disability were the main reasons for his heavy drinking and drug abuse. When he eventually reached the end of his tether, he attempted suicide. He summarises this extreme phase in his life with: "I learnt not to immediately blame others for my mistakes and not to lose my optimism." This attitude has also helped the entrepreneur (Kahawatte now employs

Beratungsagentur acht Teilzeit- und Vollzeitkräfte beschäftigt – darunter zwei mit Sehbehinderung –, auch bei der Bewältigung weiterer gesundheitlicher Probleme. Lebensbedrohlich ist eine Krebserkrankung im Unterleib, die bei ihm diagnostiziert wird, als er 24 Jahre alt ist. Operation und Chemotherapie retten ihm das Leben. Später kommen Hüftprobleme dazu, mittlerweile hat Kahawatte zwei künstliche Hüftgelenke. Gestoppt haben diesen Mann weder sein mittlerweile auf nur noch fünf Prozent geschrumpftes Sehvermögen noch die lange zurückliegende Krebserkrankung oder die andauernden Gehbeschwerden – und auch nicht die Absagen auf die mehr als 250 Bewerbungen, die Kahawatte damals im Anschluss an sein Studium als Betriebswirt der Fachrichtung Hotellerie und Gastronomiemanagement geschrieben hatte. In seinen Bewerbungen hatte er nicht nur seine Abschlussnote 1,9, sondern stets auch den Grad seiner Behinderung angegeben.

Nach seinem Studienabschluss macht er daher aus der Not eine Tugend und nutzt seine Fähigkeit, schwere Schicksalsschläge zu überwinden, für den Schritt in die Selbstständigkeit als Personal Coach und Trainer. Inzwischen unterrichtet er außerdem an Bildungsinstitutionen und ist Berater für Großkonzerne und mittelständische Unternehmen. »Das, was ich trotz der vielen Widerstände erreicht habe, macht mich zufrieden. Ich habe im Rahmen meiner Möglichkeiten das Optimale rausgeholt«, bilanziert der Unternehmensberater stolz. Das gelte auch für seine Fitness. Die Zeit des körperlichen Raubbaus sei vorbei. Zweimal am Tag betreibt Kahawatte Sport, geht schwimmen und zum Krafttraining. Die vegane und ayurvedische Küche helfe ihm zusätzlich dabei, sein Normalgewicht zu halten. Das Essen auf Ayurveda-Grundlage hatte ihm seine Großmutter in Sri Lanka nahegebracht, die die Familie damals regelmäßig in den Sommerferien besuchte. Der Fast-Erblindete hat seine Kenntnisse der Ayurveda-Küche inzwischen auch in einem Kochbuch veröffentlicht.

Auf das Thema Rassismus hat Kahawatte einen anderen Blick als Menschen ohne Handicap. Rassismus ist für ihn vergleichbar mit Behindertenfeindlichkeit: »Ein Mensch wird aufgrund eines Merkmals darauf reduziert, und ihm wird der Zugang zu Leistungen, die er erbringen könnte, versperrt.« Dem will Kahawatte mit dem Engagement des von ihm gegründeten Vereins Saliya Foundation e. V. etwas entgegensetzen. Der Verein begleitet behinderte Menschen auf ihrem Weg in den ersten Arbeitsmarkt und bietet Unternehmen eine Inklusionsberatung an. Die Arbeit soll ausgeweitet und in eine zu gründende Saliya Consulting Group ausgelagert werden. »Alles, was ich in meinem Leben gemacht habe, würde ich genauso wieder machen«, sagt der Wahlhamburger selbstbewusst und ergänzt: »Ausgrenzung, Diskriminierung und meine Gegenwehr sind die Wiege meiner Stärke.« Stärke und Mut schätzt er auch an seinen persönlichen Helden Muhammad Ali, Martin Luther King, Josephine Baker und Nelson Mandela.

Das Selbstbewusstsein seines noch unsicheren zwölfjährigen Ichs würde er stärken, indem er sich selbst fragen würde, warum er nicht weiterwisse. »Ich würde ihm raten, seine Meinung zu sagen, denn ich selbst löse ganz viele Probleme mit Klarheit und Direktheit.« Mehr über diese Strategie, die es einem Menschen ermögliche, trotz aller Widrigkeiten ein erfülltes Leben zu führen, will der Autor in der geplanten Fortsetzung seiner Autobiografie verraten, endet die erste doch mit dem Jahr 2006. »Ich möchte mein Leben mit anderen teilen und hoffe, dass auch dieses Buch wieder auf die Leinwand gebracht wird.«

eight part-time and full-time staff at his consulting agency, including two with visual impairments) to cope with other health problems. He was diagnosed with life-threatening cancer at 24. Fortunately, surgery and chemotherapy saved his life. Later, he developed hip problems – and Kahawatte now has two artificial hip joints. Neither his eyesight, which has now shrunk to just 5%, nor his long-past cancer and ongoing mobility issues have stopped this man. Nor did the over 250 rejections Kahawatte received when applying for jobs after completing his degree in business administration in the hotel and catering sector. In each of his applications, he not only stated his final grade of 1.9 (equivalent to a B), but also the extent of his disability.

After graduating, he therefore made a virtue of necessity and used his ability to overcome some of life's greatest challenges to step into self-employment as a life coach and personal trainer. Meanwhile, he also teaches at various educational institutions and is a consultant for large and medium-sized companies. "I'm satisfied with the things I've achieved in the face of so many obstacles. I've done the best I can within the limits of my abilities," sums up the management consultant proudly. This also applies to keeping fit. The time of physical exhaustion is over; Kahawatte now exercises twice a day, goes swimming, and does weight training. Vegan and Ayurvedic cuisine also help him to maintain a healthy weight. He was taught to eat an Ayurveda-based diet by his Sri Lankan grandmother, who used to visit the family regularly during the summer holidays. The nearly blind man has since channelled his knowledge of Ayurvedic cooking into his own cookbook.

Kahawatte has a different view of racism than people without disabilities. For him, racism is not dissimilar to discrimination against those with disabilities: "A person is reduced to a single characteristic and they're denied access to services that they could provide themselves." Kahawatte wants to counter this through the work of his association, Saliya Foundation e.V. The association helps those with disabilities to enter the workplace and offers companies guidance on diversity and inclusion. There are now plans to expand this work, which will be outsourced to the soon-to-be-founded Saliya Consulting Group. "Everything I've done in my life, I'd do again in exactly the same way," asserts Kahawatte, now living in Hamburg, adding: "Exclusion, discrimination and my resistance form the cradle of my strength." He also values the strength and courage of his personal heroes: Muhammad Ali, Martin Luther King, Josephine Baker and Nelson Mandela.

He would shore up his insecure twelve-year-old self's confidence by asking him why he was stuck: "I would advise him to speak his mind because I solve a lot of problems through clarity and directness." The author plans to reveal more about this strategy, which he says empowers a person to live a fulfilling life against all odds, in the planned sequel to his autobiography, which recounted his life up to 2006: "I want to share my life with others and hope the events of this book will also be brought to the big screen."

Akosua Ina'mi Aset

YOGALEHRERIN

»Ich glaube an die magische Kraft der Liebe. Selbstliebe ist der Schlüssel zu wahrem Mitgefühl, und wenn das gelebt wird, kann es Wunder bewirken.«

Akosua Aset ist eine Trendsetterin. Mit 16 Jahren fängt sie an, ihre Haare nicht mehr in Zöpfen zu zähmen, sondern Afrolook zu tragen. Andere aus ihrem Umfeld tun es ihr nach. Mit 20 wird sie Veganerin und erntet Unverständnis im Freundeskreis. Heute leben viele ihrer Freundinnen, die früher ihre vegane Ernährungsweise ablehnten, ebenfalls vegan oder vegetarisch. »Ich habe auch Kemetic-Yoga nach Deutschland gebracht, und die Nachfrage steigt«, so die Yogalehrerin. Bei Kemetic-Yoga geht es um die Verbindung zur eigenen inneren Göttlichkeit. Vieles von dem, was sie tut, beeinflusst andere, es auch mal auszuprobieren. Bereits während ihrer Schulzeit beginnt die 1985 in Miami Beach geborene Aset, die als Baby mit ihrer Familie nach Deutschland gekommen war, mit Yoga. Dass sie die Kombination aus Sport und Lebensphilosophie eines Tages zum Beruf machen wird, ist da noch nicht abzusehen.

Nach der Schulzeit absolviert die Kielerin eine Ausbildung zur sozialpädagogischen Assistentin und beginnt anschließend, Sozialpädagogik zu studieren. Aset: »Soziale Arbeit lässt sich gut mit Bewegung und Yoga vereinen. Ich wollte immer schon Menschen mit Migrationshintergrund, vor allem Schwarze Mädchen und Frauen, unterstützen.« Als sie schwanger wird, rückt jedoch erst einmal die Familiengründung in den Vordergrund. Sie heiratet und bricht das Studium ab. An ihrer persönlichen Weiterentwicklung arbeitet sie dennoch: 2012 lässt sich die junge Mutter auf Jamaika zur Kemetic-Yogalehrerin ausbilden. Eineinhalb Jahre lebt sie auf der Karibikinsel, von der ihre Familie stammt, und erinnert sich gern zurück: »Auf Jamaika war ich nach einer Zeit eine unter vielen. Ich habe dort bewusst sehr einfach gelebt, zum Beispiel das Wasser vom Fluss geholt. Der Aufenthalt hat mich sehr viel komplexer gemacht.« Ihr Wunsch, sich persönlich und fachlich weiterzuentwickeln, ist auch nach der Rückkehr stark, und so nimmt sie während der Schwangerschaft mit ihrem zweiten Kind an einer Fortbildung zur Gesundheits- und Ernährungsberaterin teil.

Dass ihre eigene Mutter, als sie nach Deutschland kam, einen gewissen Nachholbedarf in puncto Konsum gehabt habe, ihr materielle Dinge wichtig gewesen seien, könne sie gut verstehen, sagt aber über sich selbst: »Ich kümmere mich mehr um meinen Körper und meine Seele.« Besonders nachdem ihr damaliger Ehemann handgreiflich wird und sie ein halbes Jahr braucht, um ihre Angst vor der Übernahme der alleinigen Verantwortung für sich und ihre inzwischen drei Kinder zu überwinden und ihn zu verlassen. Ihre Freundinnen bestärken sie darin, den Mut dazu aufzubringen. Eine nimmt sogar zeitweise die vierköpfige Familie bei sich auf. »Ich bin dankbar für meine tollen Freundinnen, für meine Mutter, die mich unterstützt, wo sie kann, und dafür, dass ich früh im Leben den Weg zur Kemetic-Yoga gefunden habe – und für meine drei Kinder, auf

YOGA INSTRUCTOR

"I believe in the magical power of love. Self-love is the key to genuine compassion and can work miracles when you put it into practice."

Akosua Aset is a trendsetter. At sixteen,, she decided she would no longer tame her hair with braids; instead, she would wear her afro out. Others around her soon followed her lead. At twenty,, she became vegan and was met with incomprehension from her peers. Today, many friends who had previously rejected her vegan diet are also vegan or vegetarian. "I also brought Kemetic yoga to Germany – and demand for it is surging," says the yoga instructor. Kemetic yoga is all about connecting to your inner divinity, and much of what she does has convinced others to try that out too.

Aset was born in Miami Beach in 1985 and arrived in Germany with her family as a baby. The expert yogi started practising yoga during her school years. At the time, she had no idea that the practice, which combines athleticism with a way of life, would one day become her job. After leaving school, the Kiel local trained as a social pedagogical assistant and embarked on a degree in social pedagogy. According to Aset: "Social work can be neatly combined with movement and yoga. I always wanted to help people with an immigrant background, and especially Black girls and women." Yet when she found out she was pregnant, starting a family became her main priority. Aset got married and dropped out of university, but she never stopped working on her personal development. In 2012, the young mother trained as a Kemetic yoga instructor in Jamaica. She lived on the Caribbean island (where her family has its roots) for eighteen months, and looks back on that time fondly: "After a while in Jamaica, I was just one of many. I deliberately lived very simply there, fetching my water from the river, for instance. My time there made me a much more complex person." Her desire to develop personally and professionally didn't wane on her return, so she completed further training to become a health and nutrition coach while pregnant with her second child.

Aset can well understand that, on arrival in Germany, her mother felt a certain need to 'catch up' and that material things were important to her. However, she has other priorities: "I prefer to take care of my body and soul." Especially after her then-husband became violent, it took her six months to conquer her fear of leaving him and becoming solely responsible for herself and her children (of which there were now three). Her friends helped her to summon the courage to do so, and one of them even took the family of four in for a while. "I'm grateful for my wonderful friends, for my mother, who supports me wherever she can, for the fact that I found my way to Kemetic yoga early in life, and for my children, of whom I'm also very proud." The three little ones didn't have an easy time of the separation and prior domestic incidents.

die ich auch stolz bin.« Die zwei Kleinen und der Älteste hätten es mit der Trennung und den Vorfällen zu Hause nicht leicht gehabt.

Manchmal sei sie überrascht darüber, wie sie es schaffe, Kindererziehung, Yogakurse und die Werbung dafür auf Social Media sowie ihr wiederaufgenommenes Studium tatsächlich unter einen Hut zu bringen. »Mein Studium hätte ich gern schon eher abgeschlossen, auch wenn ich zwischenzeitlich viele andere Dinge kennengelernt habe. Jetzt mache ich das für meinen Seelenfrieden.« Zu diesen anderen Dingen, die für Aset eine größere Bedeutung bekommen haben, gehört neben Gedichteschreiben und Tarotkartenlegen die Musik. 2018 sind sie und ihr damaliger Ehemann Mitglieder einer Band, die Studioaufnahmen macht und Auftritte in Belgien, Österreich und der Schweiz hat. Singen, Trommeln und Gitarrespielen integriert Aset auch heute noch so oft es geht in ihren Alltag.

Sie ist froh darüber, dass sich als Lehrerin für Yoga und Meditation beruflich Geld verdienen lässt. »Spiritualität wird heute nicht mehr so abgetan. Es gibt bei Frauen und Männern ein größeres Bewusstsein für feminine Energie und die Verbindung zur Seele – überall auf der Welt. Das motiviert mich«, sagt sie. Sich selbst bezeichnet sie am liebsten als Heilerin, die auf der Reise sei, sich selbst zu heilen, die gerne anderen begegne und sie ein Stück weit mitnehme. Und währenddessen versuche sie, anderen zu helfen. »Wo ich hinwill, gibt es keine Frau, die das macht, was ich mache und machen möchte. Mein Vorbild ist eher abstrakt, steht für Weisheit, Intuition, Liebe, Magie und Mütterlichkeit. Es ist die ägyptische Göttin Isis.« Deren ursprünglicher Name ist Aset, den sie als Nachnamen trägt.

Frauen insgesamt bewundert sie. »Sie sind meine Heldinnen. Sie ziehen Kinder alleine auf, stellen Unternehmen auf die Beine, unterstützen ihre Männer. Frauen wird viel zu wenig gesagt, wie toll sie sind«, findet Aset. Sie sei schon als Kind froh gewesen, ein Mädchen zu sein – das einzige Mädchen, sogar das einzige Kind überhaupt mit einem Migrationshintergrund an ihrer weiterführenden Schule. Rassismus habe sie dort am prägnantesten von Lehrern erfahren, die sie für dumm erklärt oder des Dealens mit Drogen verdächtigt hätten. »Und das, obwohl ich weder Alkohol getrunken noch Zigaretten geraucht habe, geschweige denn sonstige Drogen überhaupt kannte.« Heute, mit genügend Abstand, hat sie eine Erklärung für rassistische Kommentare: »Ich sehe das nicht als etwas Persönliches. Es ist ein Komplex von Menschen, die sich selbst nicht lieben und Angst haben, mit ihren eigenen Unzulänglichkeiten konfrontiert zu werden.« Sie selbst verbindet Positives mit ihrer Hautfarbe, findet sie schön. Und sie ist stolz auf ihre afrikanische Herkunft, auf die Musik, die Kleidungskultur, das Essen, die Königreiche und die Sprachen.

Die zwölfjährige Akosua saugt bei einem Jamaika-Aufenthalt die Rap- und Hip-Hop-Musik auf, die ihre Cousins und Cousinen hören, und bringt sie mit in ihre deutsche Schulklasse. »Erst fanden das alle komisch und dann total cool.« Schon damals hat sie bei einem Trend die Nase ganz vorn. Wenn sie ihrem zwölfjährigen Ich Mut zusprechen könnte, würde das so klingen: »Du bist dir noch nicht bewusst, dass du in vielen Dingen Vorreiterin bist. Weiter so!«

Sometimes, Aset is genuinely astonished at how she has managed to combine raising children, running yoga classes, advertising her classes on social media, and resuming her studies: "I'd have liked to have finished my degree earlier, even though I got to do lots of other things in the meantime. Now I'm doing it for my own peace of mind." Alongside poetry writing and tarot card reading, the things that have taken on greater meaning for Aset include music. In 2018, she and her ex-husband were in a band, which had made studio recordings and performed in Belgium, Austria and Switzerland. Today, Aset continues to incorporate singing, drumming and guitar-playing as often as she can into her everyday life.

She's glad that she can make a living teaching yoga and meditation. "Today, spirituality is no longer dismissed like it once was. Men and womenall over the world have a greater awareness of feminine energy and the connection to the soul. That's what motivates me," she says. She most likes to describe herself as a healer who's on a journey to heal herself, and who likes to meet others and bring them a little along the way with her. In the meantime, she tries to help other people: "Where I want to go, there's no woman who does what I do or what I want to do. My role model is rather abstract and represents wisdom, intuition, love, magic and maternalism. She's the Egyptian goddess Isis." The deity's original name was Aset – the name the yoga instructor has taken as her surname.

Aset admires women in general. "They're my heroes. They raise children alone, get companies off the ground, and support their husbands. Women aren't told often enough how wonderful they are," she maintains. Even as a child, the yogi was delighted to be a girl – the only girl and, indeed, the only child at her secondary school with an immigrant background. At school, she experienced the most striking racism from her teachers, who told her she was stupid or suspected her of dealing drugs, "even though I'd never drunk alcohol or smoked a cigarette, let alone knew anything about drugs!" Today, with the benefit of time and space, she has an explanation for these racist comments: "I don't take it personally. It's a complex common to those who don't love themselves and who are scared of being confronted with their own shortcomings." As for herself, she only associates positive things with her skin colour and thinks it's beautiful. And she's proud of her African heritage – the music, the fashion, the food, the kingdoms, and the languages.

Twelve-year-old Akosua soaked up the rap and hip-hop her cousins were listening to in Jamaica and brought them back to her German school friends: "At first they found it very strange, and then really cool". Even back then, she was ahead of the curve. If she had the chance to offer words of encouragement to her twelve-year-old self, she'd say: "You don't know yet in just how many ways you're going to be a trailblazer. Keep going!"

Daniel & Adrian Sousa

UNTERNEHMER

Daniel Sousa: »Ich glaube daran, dass das Leben ein großer Hindernislauf ist. Es kann sein, dass man stolpert oder sogar hinfällt. Wichtig ist es, wieder aufzustehen und weiterzulaufen, um am Ende mit breiter Brust die Ziellinie zu überqueren.«

Adrian Sousa: »Wenn man sich auf das Gute konzentriert, wird das Gute besser.«

Wenn Daniel und Adrian Sousa auf ihre Jugend zurückblicken, wären sie gern etwas »straighter« gewesen. »Ich war immer ein Unruhestifter, was sich nicht gerade positiv auf meine schulischen Leistungen ausgewirkt hat«, erinnert sich Adrian, 1994 geboren. Sein sieben Jahre älterer Bruder Daniel weiß erst heute die vielen Möglichkeiten, Einblicke, das Wissen aus der Schule zu schätzen. Doch so geht es wohl vielen Menschen. Daniel und Adrian Sousa sind dennoch erfolgreiche Unternehmer geworden. Im norddeutschen Uetersen betreiben sie seit 2019 eine Kaffeerösterei und einen Shop. Außerdem bieten sie Barista-Kurse sowie Kaffee-Tastings an und haben eine Kooperation mit einem Hersteller für Kaffeemaschinen geschlossen. Ihre Erfahrungen, die sie auf ihren nicht immer geradlinigen Wegen dorthin gemacht haben, kamen ihnen dabei zugute, wie sie meinen. Auch ihre Kraft und ihr Mut, ihr Ziel zu verfolgen, Neues zu schaffen und das Beste aus der jeweiligen Situation zu machen, habe ihnen dabei geholfen.

Die beiden wachsen zusammen mit einer jüngeren Schwester im wohlhabenden Hamburger Stadtteil Eppendorf auf. Ihre Eltern stammen von den Kapverdischen Inseln. Der Vater war schon Mitte der 1960er-Jahre als Seefahrer zu Blohm+Voss gekommen, die Mutter kam 1984 als 15-Jährige nach Deutschland, heiratete den 19 Jahre älteren Mann mit 18. »Der Altersunterschied war schon sehr groß. Vielleicht war das auch der Grund, warum die Ehe irgendwann gescheitert ist«, erzählt Daniel Sousa. Er und sein Bruder besuchen in Eppendorf die Grund-, Daniel dort später auch die Gesamtschule. »Unsere Schulzeit war schon von Weißen geprägt, weil es damals einfach noch nicht so viele Schwarze Menschen in Hamburg gab«, erinnert sich Adrian. Gelitten habe er darunter nicht, sich nur manchmal über die Unwissenheit von Mitschülern und deren Eltern gewundert. »Für mich ist Rassismus etwas Außerirdisches, von Menschen Gemachtes, das ich nicht verstehen kann, das du nicht verstehen willst«, fügt Daniel in breitem Hamburgisch hinzu. Er sei froh, dass Menschen mit unterschiedlichem Hintergrund in Deutschland immer selbstverständlicher werden.

Daniel macht den Realschulabschluss, zum Abitur reicht es damals nicht. »Einfach weil ich Schule nicht ernst genommen habe«, sagt er. Er wechselt auf eine Handelsschule, macht dann auf einem Wirtschaftsgymnasium Abitur und schließt danach ein Betriebswirtschaftsstudium mit dem Bachelor ab. Immer wieder macht er Praktika, auch bei großen Unternehmen wie dem Versandhändler Otto Group. »Das war toll, aber ich

ENTREPRENEURS

Daniel Sousa: "I believe that life is a giant obstacle course. You might well stumble or even fall down; the important thing is to get back up and keep running, so that you can proudly cross the finish line."

Adrian Sousa: "If you focus on the good, the good gets better."

When Daniel and Adrian Sousa look back on their youth, they say they'd have liked to have been a little 'straighter': "I was always a troublemaker, which didn't exactly have a positive impact on my school performance," recalls Adrian, born in 1994. Likewise, his brother Daniel, seven years older, only now appreciates the many opportunities, insights, and knowledge he gained from school. But that's probably how it is for many people. Despite this, Daniel and Adrian Sousa have become successful entrepreneurs. The pair have been running a coffee roastery and shop in Uetersen, northern Germany, since 2019. They also offer barista courses and coffee tastings, and have now entered a partnership with a coffee machine manufacturer. They believe that the experiences they've had on their not-so-linear path to success have only benefited them in the long run. Their strength and courage in pursuing their goal, creating something new, and making the best of the situation at hand have also helped.

The Sousa brothers grew up with their younger sister in the affluent Eppendorf district of Hamburg. Their parents are from the islands of Cape Verde. Their father, a seafarer, came to work at the Blohm+Voss shipbuilding company in the mid-60s, while their mother arrived in Germany at fifteen in 1984, marrying the man nineteen years her senior when she was just eighteen. "The age gap was really rather big. Maybe that's the reason why the marriage eventually failed," says Daniel Sousa. He and his brother attended primary school in Eppendorf, and Daniel later attended a comprehensive there. "Our school days were shaped by white people because there simply weren't that many Black people in Hamburg back then," Adrian recalls. While he didn't suffer for it, he did sometimes wonder about the ignorance of his classmates and their parents. "For me, racism is something alien, something man-made that I can't and don't want to understand," Daniel adds in broad Hamburgish. He says he's glad that people from different backgrounds are becoming more and more commonplace in Germany.

Daniel completed his school-leaving certificate, but didn't then go on to obtain his Abitur – the German qualification needed to access university. "I simply didn't take school seriously enough," he says. He therefore switched to a commercial college. It was there that he finally passed his Abitur, ultimately allowing him to complete a bachelor's degree in business administration. He also did a number

habe schnell gemerkt, dass ich selbstständig arbeiten und etwas bewirken will«, erinnert er sich. Es ist ein Zufall – oder vielmehr die Liebe zu seiner heutigen Frau –, der Daniel auf die Idee einer eigenen Kaffeerösterei bringt. »Meine Frau war damals in Honduras und lebte bei der Gründerfamilie der Kaffeekooperative COMSA, mit der wir heute eng zusammenarbeiten. Ich habe dann meine Bachelorarbeit über den Aufbau einer Kaffeebar geschrieben, mit Businessplan und allem Drumherum«, erzählt er. Also entschließt er sich, es selbst zu wagen – gemeinsam mit seinem Bruder. »Wir haben uns immer super verstanden, vielleicht auch, weil wir uns lange ein Zimmer geteilt haben und gerade nach der Trennung unserer Eltern noch näher zusammengerückt sind«, sagt Daniel. Für Adrian sei er immer der große Bruder gewesen, der sich um alles kümmert.

Auch Adrian macht den Realschulabschluss, schließt eine Kochlehre ab, merkt aber schnell, dass er seine Leidenschaft nicht zum Beruf machen will. Parallel spielt er recht erfolgreich beim HSV in der A-Jugend im Profibereich Fußball. Doch sein Talent reicht nicht aus. Er hängt eine weitere Ausbildung als Speditionskaufmann dran. »Als mein Bruder mich dann fragte, ob ich bei ihm mitmache, musste ich nicht lange überlegen.« Ihre Eltern unterstützen die beiden, geben ihnen Kraft, der engere Freundeskreis ist da schon skeptischer. Doch was haben wir schon zu verlieren?, fragen sie sich. Sie sind jung und risikobereit. »Und wir leben in einem Land, das einem die Chance gibt, auch nach einer Niederlage wieder auf die Beine zu kommen«, sagt Daniel dankbar.

2017 reisen sie nach Honduras, leben in derselben Gastfamilie wie einst Daniels Frau, treffen die Kaffeebauern. »Da waren wir gleich geflasht«, erinnert sich Adrian. Für Daniel eröffnet Honduras die Möglichkeit, ein Unternehmen zu gründen, wie er es sich immer vorgestellt hat. »Wir verkaufen nicht irgendein Produkt, sondern eines, hinter dem wir zu 100 Prozent stehen, nicht nur weil wir selbst gern Kaffee trinken«, sagt er und lacht. Die Röstlich Coffee Brothers, wie Daniel und Adrian Sousa sich nennen, zahlen den Kleinbauern in Honduras weit mehr als selbst Fair-Trade-Anbieter es tun. Sie setzen auf Nachhaltigkeit, Umwelt- und Klimaschutz, vom Anbau bis zur Auslieferung mit einem Elektroauto. Und sie unterstützen soziale Projekte, bieten den Kaffeebauern die Möglichkeit, sich weiterzuentwickeln. Für Daniel und Adrian ist dies Teil ihrer sozialen Verantwortung als Bürger eines reichen Landes. Sie wollen etwas weitergeben – nicht nur im materiellen Sinne. »Ich denke, wir als Schwarze Unternehmer zeigen so, dass wir etwas bewirken können. Wir wollen auch Vorbild sein«, sagt Adrian. Sein eigenes Idol war lange der portugiesisch-kapverdische Fußballer Nani, der 2016 mit der portugiesischen Nationalmannschaft Europameister wurde und bis heute aktiv ist. »Der hat etwas gerissen, auch sozial.«

Daniel Sousa bewunderte in seiner Jugend Schwarze Stars wie den Schauspieler Will Smith oder den Basketballer Michael Jordan. Heute ist Barack Obama einer seiner persönlichen Helden. Ebenso wie seine Frau, die ihm ein neues Leben eröffnet habe, ihm den Rücken freihalte und ihn immer wieder motiviere, wenn es mal nicht so gut laufe. Wie während der Corona-Pandemie, als sich die Coffee Brothers mit Online-Verkauf und der Zusammenarbeit mit einem Hersteller von Espressomaschinen, Kaffeemühlen und Zubehör noch einmal breiter aufstellten.

Auch zu ihrer Mutter schauen die beiden jungen Unternehmer auf. Nach der Scheidung hat sie für sich noch einmal einen neuen Weg gefunden. Ihr verdanken sie, wie sie sagen, ihre Offenheit und ihre positive

of internships, including at large companies like the Otto Group mail-order company. "That was great, but I quickly realised that I wanted to work for myself and make a difference," he explains. It was pure coincidence – or rather his love for his-wife – that gave Daniel the idea of founding his own coffee roasting company. "My wife was in Honduras at the time living with the founding family of the COMSA coffee cooperative, with whom we now work closely. I then wrote my bachelor's thesis on setting up a coffee bar, business plan and all," he says. He ultimately decided to take a chance on it himself – in partnership with his brother. "We've always got along great, maybe because we shared a room for a long time, and we got even closer after our parents separated," says Daniel. To Adrian, he's always been the big brother who takes care of everything.

Adrian also got his school-leaving certificate and then went on to complete a chef's apprenticeship, but soon realised that he didn't want to turn his passion into his profession. At the time, he was also playing quite successfully in Hamburg SV's U19 professional football squad. Alas, his talent wasn't enough, so he added another string to his bow: an apprenticeship as a freight-forwarding clerk. "When my brother asked me if I would join him, I didn't have to think twice." Their parents supported them and gave them strength, but their closest friends were more sceptical. 'What have we got to lose?' they asked themselves; they were young and willing to take risks. "And we live in a country that gives you the chance to get back on your feet even after a defeat," says Daniel gratefully.

In 2017, they travelled to Honduras to meet the coffee farmers, staying with the same host family as Daniel's wife. Honduras gave Daniel the opportunity to start the kind of business he'd always dreamed of: "We're not selling any old product, but one that we stand behind 100% – and not just because we, ourselves, like coffee," he laughs. Röstlich Coffee Brothers, as Daniel and Adrian call themselves, pays small farmers in Honduras far more than fair trade suppliers do. The pair focus on sustainability and environmental and climate protection, from cultivation to delivery with an electric car. They also support social projects, offering coffee farmers the opportunity to develop and grow. For Daniel and Adrian, this is part and parcel of their social responsibility as citizens of a wealthy country. They want to pay something forward, and not just in the material sense. "I think it's a way for us as Black entrepreneurs to show that we can make a difference. We also want to be role models," Adrian says. His own idol has long been the Portuguese-Cape Verdean footballer Nani, who became a European champion with the Portuguese national team in 2016 and is still active today: "He's made waves, socially and otherwise."

In his youth, Daniel Sousa admired Black stars like actor Will Smith or basketball player Michael Jordan. Today, Barack Obama is one of his personal heroes – as is his wife, who has opened the door to a new life for him, has his back, and always motivates him when things aren't going so well. This was the case during the coronavirus pandemic, when the Coffee Brothers expanded their business with online sales and a partnership with a manufacturer of espresso machines, coffee grinders and accessories.

The two young entrepreneurs also look up to their mother. After the divorce, she forged herself a new path in life. They owe their

Einstellung, ihrem Vater Disziplin und – bei aller Lebensfreude – doch eine gewisse Ernsthaftigkeit. Und dann ist da noch Daniels 2017 geborene Tochter, die ihm einen weiteren neuen Blick aufs Leben eröffnet und ihn eine neue Form von Verantwortung gelehrt habe. Auch Adrian ist dankbar für seine kleine Nichte: »Sie ist es, die mich immer zum Lachen bringt, die ist echt crazy drauf.«

Für die beiden Jungunternehmer ist es wichtig, das Leben zu schätzen, es aber gleichzeitig nicht immer so ernst zu nehmen, den Blick für die positiven Dinge zu schärfen und selbstbewusst durchs Leben zu gehen. Ihr Rat für ihre zwölfjährigen Ichs lautet: »Verfolge dein Ziel, der Weg dahin kann auch Umwege nehmen.« Die beiden Sousa-Brüder haben ihn von klein auf intuitiv befolgt.

openness and positive attitude to her, and their discipline and a certain seriousness – despite all their joie de vivre – to their father. Then there's Daniel's daughter, born in 2017, who's given him a brand-new outlook on life and taught him a new sense of responsibility. Adrian is also grateful for his little niece: "She's the one who always makes me laugh; she's really crazy!"

For the two young entrepreneurs, it's important to appreciate life, but not to take it too seriously, to stay focused on the positive, and to move through life with confidence. Their advice for their twelve-year-old selves? "Pursue your goals – and know that your path may include a few detours." It's advice the two Sousa brothers have followed intuitively from a young age.

Dr. Stephanie Nsiah-Dosu

HUMANBIOLOGIN

»Ich glaube, dass jede und jeder eine Chance verdient hat; die Hautfarbe eines Menschen oder seine Herkunft sollten nicht ausschlaggebend sein.«

Für ihren beruflichen Weg hatte sie keine Vorbilder. Niemanden, dem sie nacheifern und an dem sie sich hätte orientieren können. Das war der Grund für Dr. Stephanie Nsiah-Dosu, 2021 den gemeinnützigen Verein YAPA Germany e. V. zu gründen. Dieser bietet Beratung und Mentoring für aufstrebende Nachwuchskräfte aus unterschiedlichen Berufsfeldern und zeigt den Nachkommen der Schwarzen Communitys anhand von Schwarzen Role Models, die beispielsweise als Zahnärzte, Anwälte oder Tischler arbeiten, Perspektiven für ihr eigenes Leben auf. »Es macht mich sehr glücklich, dass ich für einige Jugendliche eine Inspiration sein kann«, sagt die Vereinsvorsitzende. Sie erinnert sich an Erlebnisse, in denen sie sich aufgrund ihrer Hautfarbe und ihres Namens benachteiligt fühlte, und nennt den Bewerbungsprozess um eine Arbeitsstelle als Beispiel: »Wie kann es sein, dass man innerhalb von 19 Stunden eine Absage auf eine Bewerbung erhält? Es hieß wohl ›afrikanisch und tschüss‹.« Hätte jemand aus der Personalabteilung wirklich den Lebenslauf der 1989 in Ghana geborenen promovierten Humanbiologin gelesen, hätte das Unternehmen sie mit Sicherheit persönlich kennenlernen wollen.

Denn ihr Weg ist wirklich beeindruckend. Im Alter von 13 Jahren verabschiedet sich die Teenagerin von ihren Großeltern, die das Mädchen aufgezogen haben, und steigt erstmals in ihrem Leben in ein Flugzeug. Es wird ein Langstreckenflug nach Kaiserslautern, wo ihre Mutter seit einigen Jahren lebt. Kaum in der rheinland-pfälzischen Mittelstadt angekommen, beginnt zwei Wochen später die Schule. Nsiah-Dosu wird nicht altersgerecht in die siebte Klasse eingeschult, sondern in die fünfte, weil eine Bekannte aus Ghana diese besucht. Die Mutter glaubt, dies würde ihrer Tochter das Einleben erleichtern. Die aufgeweckte Hauptschülerin legt eine unglaubliche Zielstrebigkeit an den Tag. »Ich habe die deutsche Grammatik geliebt und mich immer gemeldet«, erinnert sie sich. Nach einem Jahr empfehlen die Lehrer den Wechsel aufs Gymnasium. Dort ist sie die einzige Schwarze. Die Mitschüler sind neugierig, stellen viele Fragen zu ihrer Hautfarbe. »Ich erinnere mich noch lebhaft, wie ich in der Pause im Schulhof angestarrt wurde und Schüler sich über meine Hautfarbe unterhielten. Damals verstand ich noch nicht einmal, warum ich plötzlich so im Mittelpunkt stand, außer dass ich eben Schwarz war.«

Am Ende der Schulzeit kristallisiert sich ein Berufswunsch heraus: »Ich wollte wissen, wie Krankheiten entstehen und wie man die therapeutisch behandeln kann.« Apothekerin steht zunächst ganz oben auf ihrer Wunschliste möglicher Berufsziele. Schließlich entscheidet sie sich für Biomedizin, ein Studienfach, das Überschneidungen sowohl mit Medizin als auch mit Biologie hat. Für das Studium geht sie nach London und jobbt nebenher in einer Apotheke, wo sie rezeptfreie Medikamente verkaufen darf. Während des ersten Jahres ihres Biomedizinstudiums

HUMAN BIOLOGIST

"I believe that anyone and everyone deserves a chance; the colour of a person's skin or where they come from should not be the deciding factor."

She had no role models in her chosen career, and no one to emulate or orientate towards. And that's why Dr Stephanie Nsiah-Dosu founded the non-profit association YAPA Germany e.V. in 2021. The association offers advice and mentoring for aspiring young professionals, and aims to show the Black community's next generation what opportunities exist in the professional world – with Black role models working in fields as wide-ranging as dentistry, carpentry and law. "It makes me very happy that I can serve as inspiration for some young people," says the association's chairwoman. She recalls times when she felt disadvantaged because of her skin colour and name, and cites the job application process as an example: "How is it possible for anyone to receive a rejection within nineteen hours of submitting an application? I guess it was 'African and goodbye'!" If someone from the HR department had actually read the Ghana-born PhD human biologist's CV, the company would undoubtedly have wanted to meet her in person.

Nsiah-Dosu's journey has been truly impressive. Born in 1989 and raised by her grandparents, she bid her home farewell and got on a plane for the first time in her life at just thirteen years old. Her first flight? A long-haul, one-way ticket to Kaiserslautern, where her mother had been living for several years. She had barely arrived in the Rhineland-Palatinate town before she started school two weeks later. Nsiah-Dosu was not enrolled in the seventh grade according to her age, but in the fifth grade, because it would allow her to study alongside an acquaintance from Ghana. Her mother believed this would make it easier for her daughter to settle in. The bright secondary school student demonstrated incredible determination: "I loved German grammar and always participated eagerly in class," she recalls. Within a year, her teachers recommended that she transfer to a grammar school. In her new school, she was the only Black girl. Her classmates were curious and asked lots of questions about her skin colour: "I vividly remember being stared at in the playground during break time and hearing students talking about my skin colour. At the time, I didn't even understand why I was suddenly the centre of attention, other than the fact that I was Black."

At the end of her school years, her desired career path began to take shape: "I wanted to know how diseases develop and how they can be treated therapeutically." Initially, pharmacist was at the top of her list of possible careers, however, she eventually settled on biomedicine, a field of study that overlaps with medicine and biology. She moved to London for her degree and worked part-time at a pharmacy, where she was allowed to sell over-the-counter medication. Yet

gerät sie in eine Krise. »Es fing damit an, dass wir eines der Module behandelten, die jeder vorher in der Schule gehabt hatte, nur ich hatte keine Ahnung davon«, erzählt sie. Sie weiß, dass sie diesen Rückstand aufholen muss, und der einzige Weg ist, in die Bibliothek zu gehen und fleißig zu lernen. Außerdem ist sie sich nicht sicher, in welche Richtung es nach dem Studium gehen soll. Ihr damaliger Verlobter und heutiger Ehemann Evans hilft ihr aus der Sinnkrise heraus,, indem er sie bestärkt, am Ball zu bleiben.

Mit dem Bachelorabschluss in der Tasche tauscht sie das Leben in der Weltstadt gegen ein Leben in Bielefeld. Dort lebt Evans, den sie 2015 geheiratet hatte. Doch bald schon zieht es Nsiah-Dosu nach Lübeck, um sich an der dortigen Uni einzuschreiben. Aufgrund ihres »First Class Honours«-Abschlusses (Einserdurchschnitt) kann sie das Masterstudium überspringen und gleich mit ihrer Promotion beginnen. Währenddessen wird ihr erster Sohn geboren. Um ihr den Rücken freizuhalten, zieht ihr Mann nach Lübeck um und geht ein Jahr in Elternzeit. »Kein Weg ist einfach, jede und jeder macht etwas durch, bevor sie oder er es geschafft hat. Dahinter steckt viel Arbeit. Aber mein Weg ist es, immer wieder aufzustehen, stark zu sein, bis ich da stehe, wo ich hinwill«, ist ihr Credo. »Ich bin meinem Mann sehr dankbar. Er ist wie ein Mentor für mich, mein Fels, meine größte Unterstützung, von Gott gesandt. Ohne ihn hätte ich das nicht schaffen können.«

2020 ist sie am Ziel, hat die Promotion in Humanbiologie geschafft. Der zweite Sprössling krabbelt während der Vorbereitung darauf schon unterm Schreibtisch herum. »Ich habe sogar die Geburt der beiden so geplant, dass ihre Geburtstage nur eine Woche auseinanderliegen, damit sie, wenn sie es wollen, zusammen feiern können«, lacht sie über ihre Planungsversessenheit. Überhaupt seien es ihre Kinder, die sie zum Lachen brächten. »Aller Stress verschwindet, wenn ich mit ihnen zusammen bin«, sagt die Mitarbeiterin eines medizintechnischen Konzerns, die im Bereich Clinical Affairs arbeitet. Das ist der Bereich, der sich mit allen Fragen der klinischen Anwendung eines Medizinprodukts beschäftigt. In ihrer Freizeit fährt sie gern Fahrrad und layoutet Flyer für den Verein. Auch dessen Logo hat sie entworfen.

Ihre Söhne Jadrian und Jemuel, inzwischen fünf und zwei Jahre alt, haben eine Mutter, die über sich sagt, ihre Fehler hätten sie gelehrt, niemals aufzugeben. »Man muss immer fokussiert sein und am Ball bleiben.« Manchmal sei sie überrascht über sich selbst, weil sie früh gewusst habe, worauf sie hinauswollte und begonnen habe, Kontakte zu knüpfen, obwohl ihre Eltern keine Akademiker waren und sie sich an niemandem in ihrer unmittelbaren Umgebung orientieren konnte.

»Alles, was ich geschafft habe, habe ich von Gott«, sagt Nsiah-Dosu. Bei so viel Ehrgeiz und Zielstrebigkeit vermag ein solches Bekenntnis schon zu erstaunen, doch die Humanbiologin sieht darin keinen Widerspruch: »Vor jeder Entscheidung, bei jedem Schritt bete ich, denn ich will mich nicht nur auf meine eigene Kraft verlassen.« Auch ihre Sichtweise auf Rassismus hat durchaus eine christliche Prägung: »Rassisten ziehen eine rote Linie. Sie sind voller Hass. Dabei sollten alle Menschen Akzeptanz finden, egal welcher Herkunft sie sind.« Die religiöse Erziehung kommt von ihren Eltern. »Meine Mutter hat mich gelehrt, immer zu beten und mich auf Gott zu verlassen. Sie hat den christlichen Glauben in mir verankert.« Ihre Mutter, die in Ghana als Buchhalterin gearbeitet hatte, nennt sie »meine Inspiration«. Ihrem zwölfjährigen, noch unsicheren

during her first year of biomedical studies, she found herself in crisis: "It started with us covering one of the modules that everyone had completed before at school, only I had no knowledge of it at all," she says. She knew she needed to catch up, and the only way to do that was to go to the library and study hard. What's more, she wasn't sure what direction to take after graduation. Her then-fiancé and now-husband, Evans, helped her overcome her crisis of purpose by encouraging her to keep going.

With her bachelor's degree in the bag, she traded life in a cosmopolitan city for a life in Bielefeld with Evans, whom she married in 2015. Nevertheless, Nsiah-Dosu soon felt compelled to enrol at the university in Lübeck. Thanks to her first-class honours degree (equivalent to top grades in the German system), she was able to skip her master's programme and immediately start her doctorate. Meanwhile, her first son was born. To support her career, her husband moved to Lübeck and took a year of paternity leave: "No path is easy; everyone goes through something before they make it. There's a lot of work behind every success. But my approach is to keep getting back up and to be strong until I find myself where I want to be," says Nsiah-Dosu, describing her personal credo. "I'm very grateful to my husband. He's my mentor, my rock, and my biggest supporter. He was sent by God and I couldn't have done this without him."

In 2020, she obtained her doctorate in human biology, her second child crawling around under her desk as she prepared for her defence. "I even planned their birthdays to be just a week apart, so that they can celebrate together if they want to," she laughs about her obsession with planning. In general, she says, it's her children who make her laugh. "All my stress disappears when I'm with them," says the employee of a medical technology corporation who now works in clinical affairs – an area that deals with all matters related to the clinical use of medical products. In her spare time, she likes to ride her bike and tinker with the layout of her association's flyers (she also designed its logo).

Her sons Jadrian and Jemuel, now five and two, have a mother who believes her mistakes have taught her never to give up: "You always have to be focused and stay on the ball." Sometimes she amazes herself because she knew early on what she was aiming for and started to make contacts, even though her parents were not in academia and she had no one in her immediate environment to guide her.

"Everything I have I received from God," says Nsiah-Dosu. She reveals: "I pray before every decision and with every step because I don't want to rely solely on my own strength." With so much ambition and determination, such a confession may seem surprising, but the human biologist sees no contradiction in it. Indeed, even her take on racism is influenced by her Christianity: "Racists draw a red line. They're full of hate. But all people should find acceptance, no matter their background." Her religious upbringing comes from her parents: "My mother taught me to always pray and to rely on God. She instilled the Christian faith in me." Nsiah-Dosu considers her mother, who worked as an accountant in Ghana, her "inspiration". To her uncertain twelve-year-old self, she would recommend listening to her siblings or others who could be role models… "and if there isn't one in the family, find one outside of it". Even today, she has no

Ich würde sie empfehlen, auf Geschwister oder andere Personen zu hören, die Vorbilder sein könnten. »Und wenn es kein Vorbild in der Familie gibt, such dir eins außerhalb.« Sie selbst hat auch heute noch niemanden, der für sie ein Vorbild oder ein Held beziehungsweise eine Heldin wäre. Doch als ältestes Kind in der Familie möchte sie ihren vier jüngeren Geschwistern ein Vorbild sein. Und ist es darüber hinaus für viele Jugendliche, die bei YAPA Germany Orientierung und Unterstützung finden.

one she could describe as a role model or personal hero. But as the family's oldest child, she'd like to be a role model for her four younger siblings – and a role model she surely is for the many young people who receive direction and support from YAPA Germany.

Dr. Karamba Diaby

POLITIKER

»Ich glaube an die Fähigkeit von Menschen, ihre Potenziale nutzen zu können.«

Seine Heimat liegt in ihm. So muss es jedenfalls sein, wenn das Leben voller Umbrüche ist, viele Neuanfänge einen herausfordern und man trotz viel Gegenwind den eingeschlagenen Weg fortsetzt. Wenn Heimat jedoch ein Ort auf der Landkarte ist, dann ist das für Karamba Diaby ein kleiner Küstenstaat in Westafrika und eine Stadt in Ostdeutschland. Im Senegal kommt er 1961 als viertes Kind seiner Eltern zur Welt. Als das Baby drei Monate alt ist, stirbt die Mutter. Die dritte Frau seines Vaters, die selbst einen Säugling hat, weigert sich, ihn mit aufzuziehen. Das übernehmen schließlich seine 17 Jahre ältere Schwester und deren Mann. Bis der Junge sieben Jahre alt ist, hält er die beiden für seine biologischen Eltern. Erst als sein leiblicher Vater an einer Blinddarmentzündung stirbt und ihm die Leute im Dorf deshalb ihr Beileid aussprechen, erfährt der Grundschüler von seinem Schicksal, denn Schwester und Schwager, so Diaby, hätten keinen Unterschied gemacht zwischen ihm und ihrem leiblichen Sohn. Sein Schwager sei es, der sein Leben am meisten beeinflusst habe, sagt der Sozialdemokrat heute. »Er war Analphabet und hat als Landwirt und Händler Fuß gefasst. Meine Zielstrebigkeit und meinen Fleiß habe ich von ihm.«

Diese Eigenschaften helfen der Vollwaise auch, als er im Alter von 13 Jahren seine Schwester und seinen Ziehvater verlassen muss, um an einem weit entfernten Ort die weiterführende Schule besuchen zu können. Eine ihm bis dahin wildfremde Familie nimmt ihn in ihrem Haus auf. Im Gegenzug hilft er ihr bei der Arbeit auf dem Feld, gibt nach dem Erledigen seiner eigenen Hausaufgaben den Kindern der Familie Nachhilfe und macht sie mit dem Koran vertraut. Es ist eine arbeitsreiche Zeit mit wenig Raum für Erholung. Doch schließlich kann der junge, ehrgeizige Mann vom Dorf die Ernte einholen: einen Studienplatz an der Uni in Dakar. Dort tauchen jedoch ungeahnte existenzielle Probleme auf: »Ich hatte gute Noten und als Waise ein Anrecht auf ein Stipendium, habe aber trotzdem keins bekommen. Ich spürte die Ungerechtigkeit.« Für den Studenten beginnt eine harte Zeit. Nur mit Mühe kann er seinen Lebensunterhalt bestreiten und muss andere um Unterstützung bitten. Ein Bekannter seines Bruders teilt seine Matratze mit ihm, denn für ein eigenes Zimmer im Wohnheim fehlt das Geld.

Dennoch verfolgt Diaby weiter sein Ziel, einen Studienabschluss zu erlangen. Und trotz seiner eigenen Not beginnt der Student, sich für bessere Studienbedingungen und eine bessere Ausstattung der Bibliotheken einzusetzen. Zu diesem Zweck schließt er sich einer linken studentischen Gruppierung an und kommt über diese in Kontakt mit dem Internationalen Studentenbund. So erfährt er von der Möglichkeit, dank eines Stipendiums in einem sozialistischen Land erst ein Jahr die Sprache lernen zu können und anschließend fünf Jahre zu studieren. »Die DDR war eines von mehreren Ländern, die ich als mögliche Zielländer angekreuzt habe, und ich habe mein Kreuz auch bei mehreren möglichen Studienfächern gemacht«, so Diaby. Durch ein Telegramm erfährt der Student,

POLITICIAN

"I believe in people's ability to meet their true potential."

He carries his home with him. That's how it has to be when life is punctuated by countless upheavals, challenging fresh starts and strong headwinds as you keep pushing along your chosen path. However, if Karamba Diaby's home could be pinpointed on a map, it would be both a small coastal state in West Africa and a city in East Germany. The youngest of four children, Diaby was born in Senegal in 1961. His mother died when he was just three months old – and his father's third wife, who had a newborn of her own, refused to raise him. Instead, this task fell to his sister (who was just seventeen years older than him) and her husband. Until he was seven years old, the boy believed the pair were his biological parents. It was only when his biological father died of appendicitis and the people of the village offered him their condolences that he learnt his true identity because his sister and brother-in-law had never made any distinction between him and their biological son. The social democrat believes that his brother-in-law has had the most influence on his life: "He was illiterate and gained a foothold in life as a farmer and trader. I got my work ethic and determination from him."

These qualities also helped the orphan when he had to leave his sister and father figure at the age of thirteen to attend a far-flung secondary school. He was taken in by a family who had, until then, been total strangers to him. In return, he helped with fieldwork, tutored the family's children after his chores were done, and taught them about the Qur'an. It was a busy time with little room for rest or relaxation. Nevertheless, the ambitious young villager was able to reap the reward of all his hard work: a university place in Dakar. Unfortunately, unexpected existential problems arose: "I had good grades and, as an orphan, was entitled to a scholarship, but I still didn't get one. I felt the injustice of that." It was the beginning of trying times for the student. He had difficulty earning his keep and had to ask others for support; an acquaintance of his brother shared a mattress with him because he didn't have the money for his own room in a student dorm.

Still, Diaby never lost sight of his goal: to obtain a degree. Despite his own hardships, the student began to advocate for better study conditions and library facilities. To this end, he formed a left-wing student association, through which he came into contact with the International Union of Students. This is how he learnt about the possibility of spending a year learning the language and then studying on a scholarship in a socialist country for five years. "The German Democratic Republic (GDR) was one of several countries I picked out as a possible destination, and I also marked a cross against several possible study paths," says Diaby. The student was soon informed via telegram that he'd been accepted to study electrical engineering in East Germany: "The education system is good in Senegal, so I knew

dass er in der DDR zum Studium für das Fach Elektronik angenommen worden ist. »Im Senegal ist das Bildungssystem gut, daher wusste ich von dem geteilten Deutschland, aber ich hatte keine fundierten Kenntnisse über die deutsche Gesellschaft. Die Stipendiumszusage war für mich zunächst einmal eine Befreiung von etlichen Sorgen.«

1985 betritt er das Land, das nur noch kurze Zeit existieren soll. Es folgt eine große Überraschung: Ohne Erklärung wird er für ein Chemiestudium eingeteilt und erhält nicht den ursprünglich zugewiesenen Studienplatz für Elektronik. In das völlig neue Umfeld und das komplett andere politische System der DDR zu kommen, sei schon extrem gewesen, so Diaby. Er, der gesellschaftspolitisch so aktiv gewesen war, muss sich jetzt ganz und gar zurücknehmen. Immerhin kann er sich noch als Studentensprecher im Internationalen Studentenkomitee engagieren. Gegen Ende seines Chemiestudiums erlebt er den Zerfall der DDR und die Wiedervereinigung. Diaby: »Die Wendezeit war eine Phase der Unsicherheit, eine sehr schwierige Zeit. Wir ausländischen Studenten wussten nicht, ob wir im vereinigten Deutschland bleiben können.« Er kann – und gründet mit seiner Frau Ute, die er bei einem studentischen Arbeitseinsatz in den Semesterferien kennengelernt hatte, eine Familie. 1994 wird Tochter Fatou geboren.

that Germany was divided, but I had no real knowledge of German society. The scholarship grant relieved me, first and foremost, of a great many worries."

In 1985, he thus arrived in a country that would only continue to exist for a few more years. What followed came as quite a surprise: without explanation, he was allocated to a chemistry programme instead of his original electronics programme. Diaby notes that this only added to the extreme culture shock he experienced upon entering an entirely new environment within the GDR's very different political system. After having been so socio-politically active, he now found he had to withdraw completely from active political life. Nevertheless, he could at least still be involved as a student spokesperson on the International Student Committee. Towards the end of his chemistry degree, he lived through the disintegration of the GDR and German reunification. "The reunification era was an era of uncertainty; it was a very difficult time. We foreign students didn't know if we'd be able to stay in a united Germany," explains Diaby. It turned out that he could, so he settled down and started a family with his wife Ute, whom he met on a student work placement during the semester break. His daughter, Fatou, was born in 1994.

Zwei Jahre später ist Diaby promovierter Chemiker, bekommt aber keine Arbeitsstelle. Er steht vor einer schwierigen Entscheidung. Soll er seine Stadt und seine junge Familie zurücklassen, um andernorts eine Stelle als Akademiker anzutreten? Diaby zeigt sich stattdessen zum wiederholten Male in seinem Leben flexibel und nimmt einen beruflichen Neuanfang in Kauf: Trotz des erlangten Doktortitels tritt er Jobs bei Vereinen und Verbänden in der Bildungsarbeit an. Dabei wird er in Landes-, Bundes- und EU-Projekten eingesetzt. Zwei Jahre arbeitet der junge Familienvater auch als Referent im Sozialministerium. Ehrenamtlich ist er Sprecher des Ausländerbeirats in Halle (Saale) und engagiert sich als Bundesvorsitzender der Ausländervertretungen. Die SPD wird auf ihn aufmerksam und fragt an, ob er nicht 2008 für den Stadtrat kandidieren wolle. Da ist er erst seit einigen Monaten Parteimitglied. Eingetreten war er, nachdem er eine Dokumentation über das Leben von Willy Brandt gesehen hatte. Den legendären Sozialdemokraten und Nelson Mandela nennt Diaby denn auch als Vorbilder.

»Ich dränge mich nicht nach vorne. Auch bei der Kandidatur zur Bundestagswahl hat mich ein alter Genosse gefragt«, so der Abgeordnete des Deutschen Bundestages. Diaby ist von sich selbst überrascht, wie er es als Politiker immer wieder schafft, neue Kontakte zu knüpfen und neue Gruppen von Menschen zu erreichen. Seine Aufgeschlossenheit habe aber auch zu Enttäuschungen geführt. »Ich habe daraus gelernt, nicht zu gutmütig und zu naiv im Umgang mit Menschen zu sein, die ich neu kennenlerne.«

Diaby zieht in den Stadtrat von Halle und 2013 auch erstmals in den Bundestag ein. Der Abgeordnete: »Es motiviert mich, Menschen zu erleben, die sich für die Gesellschaft engagieren und nie den Kopf in den Sand stecken.« Auch Diaby verzichtet auf die Vogel-Strauß-Politik, obwohl er als Person des öffentlichen Lebens immer wieder offen oder verdeckt rassistische Anfeindungen bis hin zu Todesdrohungen erlebt. Das lasse ihn nicht kalt, gibt er zu. Mittlerweile wird er vom Landes- und Bundeskriminalamt als bedrohte Person eingestuft und seine Wohnung geschützt. Einige Hassmails hält sein Team von ihm fern, andere bringt er zur Anzeige. »Rassismus ist ein weltweites, gesamtgesellschaftliches Problem, kein deutsches oder europäisches. Er basiert auf der Ungleichbehandlung von Menschen. Ich habe die Strategie, das immer öffentlich zu machen. Dann bekomme ich eine Welle von Solidarität, die mich stärkt.« Seine Hautfarbe spielt für den dreifachen Vater - mit Ute hat er noch Sohn Makhily Benjamin, und im Senegal lebt sein Erstgeborener Mamadou Tahirou - nach eigenem Bekunden keine Rolle. »Es sind die anderen, die das in den Mittelpunkt stellen.« Zum Beispiel die über 100 Journalistinnen und Journalisten, die aus aller Welt nach Halle kommen, nachdem der »Spiegel« über den Einzug des ersten aus Subsahara-Afrika stammenden Bundestagsabgeordneten berichtet hatte.

»Ich bin dankbar, dass ich die Möglichkeit bekommen habe, ohne finanzielle Grundlage Bildung und Studium zu genießen«, sagt der inzwischen auch dreifache Großvater, der sich über Comedians, Satire, Loriot und Otto Waalkes amüsieren kann. Seinem zwölfjährigen Ich, das unsicher ist und nicht weiß, wie es weitermachen soll, würde Diaby raten: »Probiere neue Sachen aus, und mache das, was dir Spaß macht.« Das tut auch sein reifes Ich: Seit 2020 bewirtschaften seine Frau und er einen Schrebergarten in Halle – dem Ort, den er seit langer Zeit seine Heimat nennt. Neben dem Senegal natürlich, den er immer wieder besucht, um Familienangehörige zu treffen.

Two years later, Diaby held a PhD in chemistry, but was unable to find work. He was therefore confronted with a difficult decision. Should he leave his city and his young family to accept an academic position elsewhere? Instead, Diaby showed flexibility for the umpteenth time in his life and embarked in a new direction; despite having obtained his doctorate, he accepted jobs with clubs and associations in the education sector. This saw him deployed to work on projects at the state, national and EU levels. The young father spent two years working as an assistant in the German Ministry of Social Affairs. He was also a volunteer spokesperson for the Foreigners' Advisory Council in Halle (Saale) and became the Federal Chairman of Foreigners' Representatives. He was eventually noticed by the Social Democratic Party (SPD), which asked him if he wanted to run for the city council in 2008. At the time, he'd only been a party member for a few months, having joined after watching a documentary on the life of Willy Brandt. Diaby cites both this legendary social democrat and Nelson Mandela as role models.

"I don't push myself forward into the limelight. It was an old friend who asked me when I was running for the Bundestag," says the German member of parliament. Diaby finds it astonishing how he continually makes new contacts and reaches new groups of people in his role as a politician. Yet his open-mindedness has also led to disappointment: "I've learnt not to be too good-natured and naive when it comes to new acquaintances."

Diaby joined both the Halle City Council and the German Bundestag for the first time in 2013. The politician reveals: "It motivates me to interact with people who are committed to society and never bury their heads in the sand." Diaby personally refrains from ostrich politics, although as a public figure he faces a steady stream of racist hostility, overt and covert, up to and including death threats. He confesses that he isn't unaffected by this. He's since been dubbed an 'at-risk individual' by the State and Federal Criminal Police Offices and his residence is now under police protection. His team keeps some hate mail away from him, but sometimes he chooses to report it to the police: "Racism is a global societal problem – it's not simply a German or European issue. It's based on the unequal treatment of people. My strategy is always to make everything public. Then I receive a swell of solidarity that gives me strength." By his own admission, skin colour doesn't really matter to the father of three – he later had a son, Makhily Benjamin, with Ute, while his first-born, Mamadou Tahirou, lives in Senegal: "It's always others who focus attention on it." An example of this is how over 100 journalists from all over the world arrived in Halle after German magazine Der Spiegel published an article on the first Bundestag minister to hail from Sub-Saharan Africa.

"I'm grateful that I had the opportunity to enjoy education and study without independent financial means," says the grandfather of three, who's fond of comedy, satire, and German entertainers Loriot and Otto Waalkes. Diaby would give the following advice to his twelve-year-old self, who was hesitant and didn't know how to proceed: "Try new things and do what you enjoy." Afterall, this is what he does as an adult; since 2020, Diaby and his wife have farmed an allotment in Halle – the city he's now long called home… next to Senegal, of course, where he still travels regularly to see relatives.

Bradley Iyamu

ACTING AGENCY OWNER, MUSICIAN AND DIRECTOR

"I believe that you can achieve anything. No matter how long it takes or how many times you fail, you have to stay true to your vision."

On 15 September 2016, Bradley Iyamu made film history at a Hamburg cinema, which screened the premiere of *T.H.U.G – True Hustler Under God*, the first ever entirely Afro-German film. In the comedy, the director tells the story of a gang of youths who roam the streets of Hamburg looking for money-making opportunities. "It was important to me for Black stories to finally be told in cinema," says Iyamu. "Afro-German films should no longer be considered an anomaly." It took three weeks to shoot his first feature film, which he largely financed himself. He was supported by well-known actresses like Cosma Shiva Hagen and Joana Adu-Gyamfi, who waived their fees, as well as a dozen or so friends with no acting experience whom he cast "off the street". Iyamu and his comrades-in-arms wanted to prove that their stories could resonate in Germany.

The premiere was also the birth of another ground-breaking idea. At the after party, Hamburg director Lars Becker expressed his interest in one of the amateur actors. That same evening, Iyamu decided to found an agency for Black actors and actresses. He brought Joana Adu-Gyamfi on board as a business partner and the pair began signing actors to the Black Universe Agency just a few months later. "I didn't want my people, like so many Black actors, to end up sidelined by some random casting agency," says the businessman. Instead, he wants to "push his artists forward" and make them visible. What's more, the Black Universe Agency insists that Black actors and actresses are no longer cast in clichéd roles with negative connotations. Requests from film, television and advertising are soaring, as is the number of actors and actresses signed with the agency. In setting up the business, Iyamu fulfilled a big dream of his. "I always wanted to be self-employed and own my own company," says the father of two, who's married to an educator. He says his role model and personal hero is his father, who immigrated to Germany from Nigeria in the early 80s and settled with his wife in the Hanseatic city, where he became a self-employed shipping engineer.

According to Iyamu, a recurring motif in his creative work is "hustling", a process of self-improvement that he knows well from his youth in Hamburg. His life's motto? "If you work on yourself, if you fight your way through, then no one can stop you." He's never let himself feel defeated and has always been able to rely on "his people". That's what Iyamu calls the mostly Black friends with whom he spent his childhood and teen years, both in and out of school: "We did our thing". He was very sporty, having played football and later picking up basketball. As a tall Thai boxer, he says nobody gave him any trouble. When Iyamu discovered his love of hip-hop, rap and

So nennt Iyamu seine meist Schwarzen Freunde, mit denen er als Kind und Jugendlicher zur Schule geht und nachmittags abhängt. »Wir haben unser Ding gemacht.« Er ist sehr sportlich, spielt erst Fußball, später Basketball. Als groß gewachsener Thaiboxer hat er »wenig Stress« gehabt. Als Bradley Iyamu seine Liebe zu Hip-Hop, Rap und R 'n' B entdeckt und mit Freunden im Übungsraum des Jugendzentrums eine Band gründet, ist er 14 Jahre alt.

Dafür, dass Bradley Iyamu die Schule nicht vernachlässigt, sorgt seine Mutter, eine ehemalige Polizistin. »Sie war sehr fokussiert, ihr Motto war: Erst die Schule, dann die Musik.« Nach dem Abitur studiert er Wirtschaftswissenschaften mit dem Schwerpunkt Marketing. Als sich die Band auflöst, startet Iyamu unter dem Künstlernamen Young Crhyme aka Money Mendoza eine erfolgreiche Solokarriere als Rapper. Vorbilder sind US-amerikanische Musiker wie 2Pac oder Jay-Z. Seine Songs werden von internationalen Radiostationen gespielt, die Alben vielfach ausgezeichnet. Regelmäßig tourt er durch die USA und Europa. Als »Marketing-Guru«, so erzählt Bradley Iyamu augenzwinkernd, habe er seine Musik mit dem neu erworbenen Wissen »auf ein neues Level bringen« können. Marketingkonzepte, Sponsorensuche und Werbekampagnen gehen ihm leicht von der Hand, seine Videoclips werden anspruchsvoller. Es folgen Kurzfilme und mit »T.H.U.G.« der erste Spielfilm.

Das Drehbuch für »T.H.U.G 2« liegt seit Jahren fertig in der Schublade, doch eine Filmförderung sucht er vergeblich. Hatten er und seine Mitstreiter gehofft, dass sich die Türen in die Filmwelt für afrodeutsche Regisseurinnen und Regisseure allmählich öffnen würden, sehen sie sich heute desillusioniert. Bradley Iyamu: »Es steht noch immer jemand dahinter, der uns nicht reinlässt.« So erlebt der Geschäftsmann, Musiker und Regisseur Rassismus als weißes Konstrukt, das dazu diene, alte Machtverhältnisse aufrechtzuerhalten. Wichtig sei es, diese Strukturen zu durchschauen, und sich nicht entmutigen zu lassen. Iyamu: »Ich habe so viel in petto und weiß, dass das, was ich mache, sehr vielen Menschen gefällt.« Als Reaktion auf negative und rassistische Erfahrungen in der Arbeitswelt, in der Musik- und Filmbranche hat Bradley Iyamu immer wieder den Weg der Unabhängigkeit gewählt, um seine Ziele zu verwirklichen. Denn eines weiß er sicher: »Es werden sich immer neue Türen öffnen. Man muss nur den Fuß hineinsetzen.«

Für Bradley Iyamu steht seine Hautfarbe für Stolz und Schönheit – und für die Verbindung zum Universum, dem Black Universe. Gemeinsam mit seiner Frau verfolgt er den Plan, sich einen zweiten Lebensmittelpunkt in Afrika aufzubauen und zwischen den Kontinenten hin- und herzupendeln. Seinem zwölfjährigen Ich würde er mit auf den Weg geben: »Glaub an deine Vision und zieh dein Ding durch, auch gegen Widerstände. Ein Nein ist niemals das Ende.«

R&B, he was fourteen years old – and went on to form a band with his friends in the practice room of their local youth centre.

His mother, a former policewoman, made sure that Iyamu didn't neglect his school work: "She was very focused and always said, school first, then music." After finishing secondary school, he studied business with a focus on marketing. When the band broke up, Iyamu started a successful solo career as a rapper under the stage name Young Crhyme aka Money Mendoza. His role models were US musicians like 2Pac and Jay-Z. Eventually, his songs were played on international radio stations and his albums won several awards. He also regularly toured the USA and Europe. As a "marketing guru", Iyamu says with a wink, he's been able to use the knowledge he's gained to "take his music to a whole new level". Marketing concepts, finding sponsors, and running ad campaigns came easily to him, and his video clips became increasingly sophisticated. Short films followed, culminating in *T.H.U.G*, Iyamu's first feature film.

The script for *T.H.U.G 2* has been gathering dust for years, but he's searched in vain for funding. Whereas he and his comrades-in-arms had once hoped that the film industry would gradually open its doors to Afro-German directors, they now find themselves feeling disillusioned. According to Iyamu: "There's still someone standing behind the door who won't let us in." The businessman, musician and director therefore sees racism as a white construct that serves to maintain old power relations. Nevertheless, he believes it's important to see through these structures and not to be discouraged. The determined young man says: "I have so much up my sleeve and I know that a lot of people like what I do." In response to his negative and racist experiences in the professional sphere, Iyamu has always followed an independent path to realise his music and film ambitions – because he knows one thing for sure: "New doors will always open; you just have to get your foot in there."

For Iyamu, his skin colour embodies pride and beauty – and a connection to the universe, the Black Universe. Together with his wife, he's working to create a second home base in Africa that will allow him to shuttle back and forth between the two continents. He would tell his twelve-year-old self: "Believe in your vision and do your thing, even when you meet resistance. A 'no' is never the end."

Joana Kohrs

SCHAUSPIELERIN UND INHABERIN EINER »ZEITGEIST-AGENTUR«

»Ich glaube an die Worte von Maya Angelou: ›Wenn du immer versuchst, normal zu sein, wirst du niemals erfahren, wie wundervoll du bist.‹«

Joana Kohrs sprudelt nur so vor Ideen. Sie kommen ihr »nonstop in den Sinn«, erzählt die Wahlberlinerin und lacht herzhaft. Im Auto, beim Shoppen, im Gespräch mit Freundinnen – und sogar nachts im Schlaf. Die kleineren kann sie in wenigen Tagen umsetzen, andere reifen über Jahre, und »keiner weiß, ob es am Ende etwas wird«. Dieses Grundvertrauen, mit dem die 48-Jährige durchs Leben geht, haben ihr ihre Eltern geschenkt. »Sie haben meine Ideen, und von denen hatte ich schon immer sehr viele, nie verlacht oder als Blödsinn abgetan. Im Gegenteil, sie hörten sich alles an und sagten dann: ›Ja, mach das.‹« Folglich sind es auch die beiden, von denen sie sagt, sie hätten ihr Leben am stärksten beeinflusst.

Den bisher erfolgreichsten Geistesblitz hatte sie vor über 15 Jahren auf einer der legendären Geburtstagspartys ihrer mittlerweile volljährigen Tochter. Offensichtlich kamen die Mottos – von Poolparty bis Zirkus – so gut bei Eltern und Kindern an, dass sie ganze sechs Jahre später beschloss, ihre Leidenschaft zum Beruf zu machen: Sie gründete die Agentur Fräulein Feiertag, mit der sie exklusive Kinderevents organisiert. »Wir machen alles, was Spaß bringt. Mein Auftrag ist es, andere glücklich zu machen«, sagt Joana Kohrs. »Wenn ich in die leuchtenden Kinderaugen blicke, dann weiß ich: Es hat funktioniert.« Auch in der Branche findet sie große Anerkennung: Für ihre exklusive Kinderbetreuung auf Hochzeiten wurde Fräulein Feiertag unlängst mit dem Wedding Award Germany ausgezeichnet.

Joana Kohrs liebt es, Neues auszuprobieren, und arbeitet stets an mehreren Ideen gleichzeitig. Mittlerweile ist sie nicht mehr nur im Kinderbereich tätig, sondern hat mit House of Feiertag auch eine Firma gegründet, mit der sie alle ihre neuen Ideen verwirklichen kann. Mit der Gründung dieser »Zeitgeist-Agentur« habe sie die »wunderbare Erfahrung gemacht, dass auf einmal all das zusammenpasst, was ich vorher gemacht habe«.

Kein Wunder also, dass sie jedem Menschen applaudiert, der den Mut findet, aus dem eigenen Schatten herauszutreten, um neue Wege zu gehen. »Ich finde, am Ende des Tages sind wir alle Helden, ganz gleich, ob Groß oder Klein, und ich freue mich immer wieder aufs Neue, wenn ich vor allen Dingen junge Menschen auf ihrer persönlichen Lebensreise begleiten darf.«

Als »waschechte Hamburger Deern« bezeichnet sich Joana Kohrs, die in der Hansestadt als Tochter eines ghanaischen Computerexperten und einer Kosmetikerin aufwuchs. Bereits während der Schulzeit entwickelt sie ihre Liebe zum Tanz, nimmt Unterricht in Ballett und Jazzdance und unterrichtet später selbst. Nach dem Abitur entscheidet sie sich für ein

ACTRESS AND OWNER OF A "ZEITGEIST AGENCY"

"I believe in the words of Maya Angelou: 'If you are always trying to be normal, you will never know how amazing you can be'."

Joana Kohrs is bubbling over with ideas. They come to her "nonstop", laughs the adoptive Berlin resident heartily – in the car, when shopping or talking to friends, and even at night as she sleeps. While she can execute the smaller ones in just a few days, others mature over a number of years and "no one knows whether or not something will come of them in the end". The 48-year-old approaches life with a deep-rooted confidence instilled in her by her parents: "They never laughed at my ideas – of which I had many, even then – and never dismissed them as nonsense. On the contrary, they always listened to everything and then said: 'Yes, go for it'." Consequently, Kohrs says her parents are her greatest influences.

She had her most successful flash of inspiration more than fifteen years ago at one of her now-adult daughter's legendary birthday parties. Apparently, the themed parties – from pool party to circus – went down so well with parents and children that six years later she turned her passion into a profession. She thus founded the Fräulein Feiertag agency, through which she organises exclusive children's events. "We do anything and everything fun. It's my mission to make others happy," says Kohrs. "When I see the children's eyes light up, I know I've done my job right." The industry has also recognised her good work; Fräulein Feiertag was recently honoured with the Wedding Award Germany for its exclusive childcare provision at weddings.

Kohrs loves to try out new things and is always working on several ideas at once. She's now branched out from the children's sector and founded a second company, House of Feiertag, which will allow her to breathe life into all of her latest ideas. With the launch of this so-called "zeitgeist agency", she's had the "wonderful experience" of suddenly being able to combine all the things she's done in the past.

It's therefore no surprise that she applauds anyone who finds the courage to step out of their own shadow and tread a new path: "At the end of the day, I think we're all heroes, big and small, and I'm always especially happy to guide young people on their personal hero's journeys."

Kohrs, the daughter of a Ghanaian computer expert and a beautician, was raised in Hamburg and describes herself as a "true denizen" of the port city. She discovered a love of dance while still at school, taking ballet and jazz classes, and later taught herself. After completing secondary school, she decided to study dance education. She also discovered the stage early on, first in musicals like *Little Shop of Horrors* and *Sweet Charity,* and later at a Hamburg children's

Studium der Tanzpädagogik. Auch die Bühne entdeckt sie früh für sich: erst in Musicals wie »Little Shop of Horrors« und »Sweet Charity«, dann in einem Hamburger Kindertheater als Regieassistentin für das Stück »Neue Punkte für das Sams«. Während sie noch im Examen schwitzt, wird ihr die Rolle der Krankenschwester Hannah Akyaa in der TV-Serie »Alphateam – Die Lebensretter im OP« angeboten, die der Vater einer Musical-Kollegin ihr auf den Leib geschrieben hat. Unter ihrem Mädchennamen Joana Adu-Gyamfi steht sie fortan in vielen TV-Produktionen und Spielfilmen vor der Kamera, vom ARD-»Tatort« und -»Polizeiruf« bis zu »Soulkitchen«, dem Kinoerfolg des Hamburger Kultregisseurs Fatih Akin. Bereits Ende der 1990er-Jahre gründet sie mit Freunden eine Agentur für Schwarze Models, Sänger und Tänzer und steigt 2017 in die Schauspielagentur ihres Freundes Bradley Iyamu mit ein: die Black Universe Agency.

Aus dem Scheinwerferlicht hat sich Joana Kohrs heute weitestgehend zurückgezogen. »Es ärgerte mich zunehmend, dass Schwarze Schauspielerinnen meist als Prostituierte, Putzfrau oder Asylbewerberin besetzt wurden«, erzählt sie. Das habe sich jedoch mit der Black-Lives-Matter-Bewegung ein wenig verändert. Einen »bescheuerten Akzent« vorspielen, der die Figur zudem als einfältig abstempelt, und Klischees bedienen? »Das macht die Community der Schwarzen Schauspielerinnen und Schauspieler heute nicht mehr mit«, sagt die Geschäftsfrau.

Mit rassistischen Erfahrungen ist Joana Kohrs groß geworden. Mehr erzählen möchte sie nicht, zu schmerzhaft seien die Erinnerungen. Jedoch hätten ihr Humor und Sarkasmus immer wieder geholfen, nicht zu verzweifeln. Ob abschätzige Blicke in Oper und Ballett oder abwertende Kommentare im Alltag: »Wenn mir jemand blöd kommt, mache ich den Mund auf«, sagt sie selbstbewusst. Sich zu behaupten, das habe ihr die Mutter vorgelebt. So erinnert Joana sich an eine gemeinsame S-Bahn-Fahrt, als eine weiße Passantin der Mutter völlig unverblümt ins Haar griff. Diese reagierte, indem sie bei der Frau dasselbe tat. »Interessant, wie sich plötzlich das gesamte Bahnabteil über das Verhalten meiner Mutter aufregte«, kommentiert Kohrs lakonisch.

So verbindet Joana Kohrs mit ihrer Hautfarbe neben Schönheit vor allem Stolz. »Wir tragen eine unsichtbare Krone. Egal wie oft uns Knüppel zwischen die Beine geworfen werden: Wir stehen immer wieder auf. Und obwohl wir Sklaverei und Unterdrückung erlebt haben und unsere Länder ausgebeutet wurden, sind wir immer noch da.« Auch sie selbst habe gelernt, berufliche und persönliche Rückschläge wegzustecken, und bezeichnet sich selbst als »Stehaufmännchen«. Mit dem für sie typischen »Hilft ja nichts!« richtet sie den Blick in die Zukunft und hadert nicht mit Vergangenem. Kohrs: »Solange ich für eine Sache brenne, mache ich weiter.«

Folgende Worte würde sie ihrem zwölfjährigen Ich mit auf den Weg geben: »Ich kann dir nicht versprechen, dass es besser wird. Aber ich kann dir sagen, dass es anders wird. Je älter du wirst, desto stärker kannst du eine Veränderung mit beeinflussen.«

theatre, where she was assistant director for the play *Neue Punkte für das Sams* ('New Spots for the Sams'). While she was still sweating through her exams, she was offered the role of nurse Hannah Akyaa in the TV series *Alphateam – Die Lebensretter im OP* ('Alphateam – The Life-Saving Surgeons'), which the father of a musical colleague had written especially for her. From then on, she appeared under her maiden name, Joana Adu-Gyamfi, in a myriad of TV productions and feature films, from broadcaster ARD's crime dramas *Tatort* and *Polizeiruf* to *Soulkitchen,* the hit film by Hamburg cult director Fatih Akin. In the late 90s, she founded an agency for Black models, singers and dancers with her friends and, in 2017, she joined her friend Bradley Iyamu's Black Universe acting agency..

Today, Joana Kohrs has largely withdrawn from the spotlight: "It increasingly annoyed me that Black actresses were mostly cast as prostitutes, cleaners or asylum seekers." However, she says that changed somewhat as the Black Lives Matter movement gained momentum. Pretending to have a "stupid accent", leading to your character being thought of as simple-minded and reinforcing stereotypes? "The Black community of actors doesn't do that anymore," asserts the businesswoman.

Kohrs experienced a lot of racism growing up. She's unwilling to speak more on this subject, explaining that the memories are too painful. Nevertheless, humour and sarcasm have always helped her to avoid despair. Whether it was disparaging looks at the opera and ballet or derogatory comments in everyday life: "If anyone gives me trouble, I open my mouth," she says, a confident gleam in her eye. It was her mother who taught her to stand up for herself. Joana remembers a ride on the tram when a white passenger simply grabbed her mother's hair. Her mother responded by doing the same back to the woman. "It was interesting how the whole train carriage suddenly got upset about my mother's behaviour," Kohrs comments laconically.

Meanwhile, Kohrs not only associates her skin colour with beauty but, above all, with pride: "We wear an invisible crown. No matter how many times we're brought to our knees, we always get back up again. And even though we've experienced slavery and oppression and our lands have been exploited, we're still here." She, too, has learnt to overcome personal and professional setbacks and describes herself as a "rubber ball" who always bounces back. Uttering her catchphrase, "It won't help any!" she looks to the future and refuses to dwell on the past: "As long as I feel passion for something, I'll keep going."

She would tell her twelve-year-old self the following: "I can't promise you that it will get better. But I can tell you that it will be different. The older you get, the more you can help to bring about change."

Thilo Cablitz

SPOKESPERSON FOR THE BERLIN POLICE FORCE

"We're all equal. And I believe that we can also all see and accept each other as equals. We just have to want to."

For some people, life presents challenges from a very early age. Thilo Cablitz, born in Berlin in 1978 to a German mother and a Sudanese father, faced significant challenges at various points during his childhood and teen years. His parents separated when he was still a toddler and his mother cut off all contact with his father. The second-youngest of five children, Cablitz was often left to look after his little sister – even before the age of five. His mother needed help herself, so he had to take care of her too. It was a time when even basic things like hot water, food and electricity were not available. Consequently, Cablitz was often absent from school. "I ultimately had to drop out at sixteen and had terrible grades when I left," Cablitz explains candidly. Nevertheless, he enthusiastically wrote an application to join the police force… and was rejected.

He then applied to 173 companies, mainly for technical apprenticeships. Since he had no money to post his applications, he delivered each one by hand. He apparently made a good impression on the secretary of one engineering firm when he handed in his documents and she recommended that her boss invite the young man for an interview. As a result, Cablitz finally secured an apprenticeship as a technical draftsman and was able to meet his full potential; he completed the three-and-a-half-year apprenticeship a year early, worked in the profession he qualified in, went back to school on the side, and caught up on his Abitur, the German qualification giving students access to university. He was able to do this because, after state care was organised for the family, he was able to leave home at the age of seventeen – and from then on, he only had to take responsibility for himself most of the time.

After finishing his education, he considered pursuing a degree in engineering: "My brother, who was a mechanical engineer thirteen years older than me, was very influential in guiding me in that direction. He was immensely proud of me when I took the next step in my career." The pair fantasised about opening an engineering firm together – but Cablitz, for whom life had presented hurdle after hurdle, compounded by losses and experiences of everyday discrimination, couldn't shake his sense of idealism. "I needed a job that was fulfilling, where I could protect people, mitigate conflict, and challenge injustice. As a policeman I can do all of this, while also being something of a social worker, too." Cablitz therefore applied to join the police force again, this time armed with an exemplary school-leaving certificate, and was soon accepted onto a course to join the higher police service. After completing his training as a police commissioner, he was initially assigned to various roles and departments. Eventually, the passionate martial artist passed the selection process for the senior police service and began a master's degree in public administration/police management.

Ein halbes Jahr lang leitet Cablitz anschließend zwei Dienststellen in zwei Berliner Bezirken, bevor er 2016 mit der Leitung der Öffentlichkeitsarbeit im Berliner Polizeipräsidium betraut wird. Mittlerweile ist er als Pressesprecher das Gesicht der Berliner Polizei und damit einer der ranghöchsten Polizeibeamten der Hauptstadt. »In dieser Funktion kann ich der Polizei nach innen und außen eine Stimme geben. Ich kann beginnen, Dinge im Großen zu verändern, indem ich hier und dort Anstöße gebe.« Cablitz wird auch in der Polizei mit Ablehnung, Vorurteilen und Rassismus durch Kollegen konfrontiert, sei aber insgesamt sehr gut in der Behörde aufgenommen worden. Das Idealbild eines Polizisten sieht er als Motivation: »Daran muss jede und jeder arbeiten, das muss man vorleben und dadurch andere mitziehen.«

Cablitz ist Mitbegründer des Netzwerks für Vielfalt, Inklusion und Akzeptanz der Polizei Berlin. Dessen Ziele sind die Wissens- und Kompetenzvermittlung im Bereich Vielfalt, einschließlich von Maßnahmen gegen Ausgrenzung und Diskriminierung. Das Netzwerk dient aber auch als Ansprechstelle für Externe und Interne, die Rat suchen oder sich austauschen wollen. Es pflegt Kontakte zu NGOs, um deren Erfahrungen aufzunehmen und Berührungsängste gegenüber der Polizei abzubauen.

Umso bizarrer sind daher die Erfahrungen, die er bei zahlreichen Demonstrationen, bei denen er als Polizist im Einsatz ist, macht. Einige Demonstranten sehen in ihm, sobald er die Uniform trägt, nur noch den

Cablitz then headed up two police departments in two Berlin districts for six months before being entrusted with public relations at the Berlin police headquarters in 2016. Since then, he's been an official police spokesperson and the face of the Berlin police force, making him one of the highest-ranking police officers in the capital: "This role allows me to give the police a voice, internally and externally. I can start to change things on a broad scale by providing a little impetus here or there." Cablitz also faces rejection, prejudice and racism from colleagues in the police force, but says that he's been very well received overall. He sees the ideal image of a police officer as motivation: "That's something everyone has to work on; you have to set an example to inspire others to follow your lead."

Cablitz co-founded the Berlin Police Force's Network for Diversity, Inclusion and Acceptance. It aims to impart knowledge and skills surrounding diversity, including measures against exclusion and discrimination. The network also serves as a point of contact for internal and external parties seeking advice or wishing to share ideas. It maintains contacts with NGOs in order to benefit from their experiences and to reduce the public's fear of contact with the police.

This makes his experiences at numerous demonstrations where he was on duty as a police officer all the more bizarre. As soon as he puts on his uniform, some demonstrators only see him as a

representative of a "repressive power apparatus", a racist by profession, as it were. This is a bitter pill to swallow for someone like Cablitz, whose stance is crystal-clear, both privately and professionally: "Human dignity is inviolable. Unfortunately, I've had to realise that I'm perceived differently because of my skin colour – that I'm looked at differently and that I'm devalued. It doesn't matter what skin colour or heritage someone has, who you love, what you believe in, or what clothes you wear. Don't just look at someone's outward appearance! There's always a human being standing in front of you." That's his conviction, but the father of two (a daughter, 19, and a son, 8) realises that it's not one held by all of society.

His daughter is from his first marriage; the parents separated when the girl was four years old. For the sake of his child, he wanted to fight for the relationship until it was no longer possible: "It tore me apart. I was and still am infinitely sorry for her," sums up the police spokesperson. He remarried in 2013. His wife, a head teacher, shares his penchant for idealism, as do his children. The three of them are his heroes: "My family gives me support and security. And they endure everything that comes with that, even the 24/7 job of a police spokesperson. Generally speaking, his heroes are those who stand up for human equality and make the world a little better, with no regard to name or position. For him personally, these include his older brother, who died at an early age, and his maternal grandmother, also already deceased, who gave him a sense of family security. In retrospect, he would have liked to spend more time with his father, but he passed away at 55, when Cablitz was still a teenager. It was only when he visited his terminally ill father in hospital that he realised his dad had been very interested in him and would have liked to have had a closer relationship.

From his parents' separation and his own divorce, to his need to take responsibility from an early age, the family's social care case, and saying goodbye to his father and brother too soon, Thilo Cablitz accepts life's challenges calmly and collectedly. "Life can be cruel," says the Berlin native, "but it also made me who I am today. I'm at peace with myself and I like to laugh a lot." And it's hard to leave him speechless. The fact that he remains "relaxed and cheeky" even in situations like job interviews is something he sometimes marvels at. He's grateful for "my family and wonderful friends. But also for all the opportunities I've had in life, even when I've had to work for them. The opportunity the head of the engineering firm gave me back then, for example."

It goes without saying that someone who's climbed this high up the career ladder is ambitious. Cablitz would also like to see more ambition and momentum in overcoming pigeonholing, prejudice and discrimination across Germany, the EU and the wider world: "I believe that discrimination is based on the ideology that you're allowed to rise above others because they're unequal. Of course, we're different and unique individuals, but that never justifies exclusion."

Cablitz says he has no problem admitting his own mistakes. However, he finds it problematic when he's not given the chance to make up for them or, if that's not possible, to learn from them and warn others not to make the same ones. He would tell his twelve-year-old self not to assume everything is set in stone, to question things, and to fight for education against all odds, even if the challenges are great.

Delaine Pastor Kühn

ANWÄLTIN

»Ich glaube an Gott und an Gutes wie Liebe, Toleranz und Empathie.«

Am Anfang sind es nur fünf – fünf Mandate. Das ist Ende 2017 die magere Bilanz der Anwältin, die im August desselben Jahres vom heimischen Büro aus den Schritt in die Selbstständigkeit gewagt hatte. Vier Jahre später beschäftigt Delaine Pastor Kühn bereits sechs Mitarbeiterinnen und Mitarbeiter, die ihr dabei helfen, die inzwischen stark angewachsene Zahl der Mandate auszuüben. Darüber hinaus gibt es Pläne, mit einer anderen Anwältin zusammen ein weiteres Büro in Berlin aufzubauen. Kühn, die auch Dolmetscherin für die portugiesische Sprache ist: »Ich habe viel Glück gehabt in meinem Leben. Alle haben mir gesagt, dass ich nie als Anwältin in Deutschland arbeiten könne. Gott hat mich gelehrt, nicht auf die Leute zu hören und nie aufzugeben.«

1981 kommt Delaine in Rio de Janeiro zur Welt. Der Vater, ein Beamter bei der Marine, und die Mutter, eine Hausfrau, bekommen noch ein weiteres Mädchen und drei Jungen. Die Erstgeborene besucht eine Privatschule. »Die Schule war sehr einfach, nicht vergleichbar mit Privatschulen in Deutschland. Es gab dort nur zwei oder drei Schwarze. Ich habe während meiner Schulzeit sehr viel Rassismus erlebt«, erinnert sich die Juristin. An der sich anschließenden High School absolviert sie parallel zum Schulabschluss eine Ausbildung zur Laborantin. 1998 schafft sie die Aufnahmeprüfung für die Uni, an der es zu diesem Zeitpunkt nur einige wenige Schwarze gibt. Ihr Ziel ist es, Medizin zu studieren, doch erhält sie für das Fach keine Zulassung. Auf Anraten ihres Vaters schreibt die 17-Jährige sich daraufhin für Jura ein. Neben dem Studium gibt sie Unterricht in Informatik und lernt durch das Absolvieren von Praktika den Arbeitsalltag in brasilianischen Kanzleien kennen. Wie schon während ihrer Schulzeit wird sie auch in dieser Lebensphase mit Rassismus konfrontiert. Sie erzählt ein Beispiel: »Während eines Praktikums bei zwei Rechtsanwälten hat die Partnerin von einem der Chefs mir gesagt, sie habe noch nie eine Schwarze getroffen, die so gut rieche.« Die so Angesprochene, damals 20 Jahre alt, reagiert emotional. Es folgt die Angst, rausgeschmissen zu werden. Doch die Wogen glätten sich, weil die Dame sich entschuldigt.

»Ich finde es schön, dass ich mit dieser Hautfarbe geboren bin. Aber ich habe so viel Rassismus im eigenen Land erlebt. Für mich ist es viel leichter, als Schwarze in Deutschland zu leben«, ist sich Kühn sicher. »Ich bin manchmal überrascht, dass die Leute mich mögen, obwohl ich einen Akzent habe. Auch die Richter sind respektvoll und nett zu mir.« Aus Brasilien fallen ihr dagegen viele Negativbeispiele ein. So wurde sie am Strand immer wieder gefragt, aus welcher Favela sie komme. Unvergessen ist auch die unerfreuliche Begebenheit an der Privatschule ihrer Tochter, wo sie für deren Nanny gehalten wurde. Rassismus ist für sie eine Krankheit. »Ich verstehe nicht, dass Menschen andere schlecht behandeln.« Es sei eine Aufgabe für alle, Rassismus zu bekämpfen.

Ihr Mann Robert, ein Kunstlehrer, ist der Grund dafür, dass die Kulturbegeisterte ihren Lebensmittelpunkt nach Hannover verlegt. Die beiden

LAWYER

"I believe in God and in good things like love, tolerance and empathy."

In the beginning, she had just five clients. This was the meagre year-end balance sheet of the lawyer who'd dared to set up her own firm from her home office in August 2017. Four years later, Delaine Pastor Kühn already employs six members of staff to help her manage her much-expanded client portfolio. She now plans to set up another office in Berlin with another lawyer. Kühn, who's also a Portuguese interpreter, says: "I've been very lucky in my life. Everyone told me that I could never work as a lawyer in Germany. God taught me to ignore those people and to never give up."

Delaine was born in Rio de Janeiro in 1981. Her father, a naval officer, and her mother, a housewife, went on to have another girl and three boys. Their oldest child, Kühn, attended a private school. The lawyer recalls: "The school was very simple; it couldn't compare to the private schools in Germany. At the time, there were only two or three Black students and I experienced a lot of racism during my school years." After moving up to secondary school, she completed an apprenticeship as a laboratory technician in parallel to her final school exams. Later, in 1998, she passed the entrance exam for university – where, again, Black students were in the minority. Her goal was to study medicine, but she wasn't admitted to the programme. On the advice of her father, the seventeen-year-old therefore enrolled in law. Alongside her studies, she worked as an IT tutor and familiarised herself with the workings of various Brazilian law firms through internships. Just like in her school years, Kühn faced racism during this period: "During an internship with two lawyers, the partner of one of the bosses told me that she'd never met a Black woman who smelled so good." The future lawyer, who was 20 years old at the time, reacted with emotion... which led her to fear she'd be ejected from the firm. However, the dust soon settled because the lady in question apologised.

"I think it's beautiful that I was born with this skin colour, but I experienced so much racism in my own country. For me, it's much easier to live in Germany as a Black person," asserts Kühn. "I'm sometimes surprised that people like me even though I have an accent. Even the judges treat me kindly and with respect." By contrast, she can think of many negative experiences in Brazil. On the beach, for example, she was always asked which favela she came from. She also remembers an unpleasant incident at her daughter's private school, where she was mistaken for her child's nanny. For Kühn, racism is a disease: "I don't understand people who treat others badly." She believes it's everyone's responsibility to fight racism.

Her husband Robert, an art teacher, is the reason why the culture-lover transplanted her life to Hanover. The two met when the father of two daughters was on holiday in Brazil. In 2004, Kühn visited

lernen sich kennen, als der Vater zweier Töchter in Brasilien Urlaub macht. 2004 reist sie zum ersten Mal zu ihm nach Deutschland. Die beiden heiraten, 2007 kommt die gemeinsame Tochter Giovanna zur Welt. Damit Delaine das Staatsexamen machen kann, übersiedeln die drei 2008 nach Brasilien, wo ihr Mann die Leitung einer deutschen Schule übernimmt. Der Plan geht auf, und mit dem Staatsexamen in der Tasche, bewirbt sich Kühn beim deutschen Generalkonsulat, um sich mit deutschem Migrationsrecht vertraut zu machen. Sie erhält den Job und arbeitet dort von 2013 bis 2016. Insgesamt acht Jahre leben sie in dem südamerikanischen Land. Zurück in Norddeutschland ist es für die Akademikerin trotz ihrer speziellen Berufserfahrung ein »Ding der Unmöglichkeit«, eine Zulassung als Anwältin zu erhalten. »Ich war enttäuscht und in der Seele getroffen.« Doch dann erfährt sie von einer Freundin, dass es zwischen Brasilien und Portugal ein Abkommen über die gegenseitige Anerkennung von juristischen Uniabschlüssen gibt. Sie fliegt nach Portugal, erhält in dem EU-Land die Zulassung als Anwältin und später dann auch die für Deutschland.

»Menschen zu helfen, die diese Hilfe wirklich brauchen, motiviert mich sehr. Dafür bekomme ich Anerkennung und erfahre Dankbarkeit«, so Kühn. Ihr Engagement geht weit über das Berufliche hinaus. So ist sie gerade erst für die SPD Hannover-Südwest in den Stadtbezirksrat Ricklingen eingezogen. Außerdem ist sie Mitglied der Arbeitsgemeinschaft »Juristinnen in der SPD« und engagiert sich in einem Verein, der Gewalt gegen Frauen bekämpft. »Ich habe viel Energie«, lacht sie. Und einen Ehemann, der hinter ihr stehe: »Mein Mann glaubt an mich und unterstützt meine Aktivitäten.« Vorgelebt habe ihr dieses Engagement ihr Vater. »Der hat sich auch in Sozialprojekten engagiert und wollte gern, dass ich in die Politik gehe.« Diesem Wunsch folgend, hatte sie schon in Rio in der Lokalpolitik mitmischen wollen, wurde damals jedoch nicht gewählt. Neben ihrem Vater nennt sie als weitere Vorbilder Martin Luther King, Angela Merkel, wegen ihrer Durchsetzungsfähigkeit und ihrer unaufgeregten Art, und Madonna, weil die für Frauenrechte stehe.

Kühn ist stolz darauf, dass sie nie aufgegeben und sich nie beirren lassen habe. »Es ist mir egal, was die Leute sagen. Auf Kritiker allerdings höre ich, um mich selbst zu verbessern.« Selbstkritisch ist sie in dem Punkt, sich nicht genug Zeit für das Erlernen der deutschen Sprache eingeräumt zu haben. »Wenn ich gleich damit angefangen hätte, als ich das erste Mal nach Deutschland kam, wäre das für meine Arbeit einfacher gewesen.« Ihrem zwölfjährigen Ich, das nach Orientierung sucht, würde sie diesen Rat mit auf den Weg geben: »Glaube an dich selbst, gebe nie auf – und studiere Jura.«

him in Germany for the first time. The pair soon married and their daughter, Giovanna, was born in 2007. To enable Kühn to take her state exams, the family of three moved to Brazil in 2008, where her husband took over running a German school. The plan worked – and with her state exam in the bag, Kühn applied to the German Consulate General to familiarise herself with German migration law. She got the job and worked there from 2013 to 2016, ultimately living in the South American country for eight years. Back in northern Germany, it was "absolutely impossible" for the academic to be recognised as a lawyer, despite her very particular professional experience: "I was disappointed; it wounded my soul deeply." However, she then learnt from a friend that there's an agreement between Brazil and Portugal to mutually recognise each other's law degrees. She flew to the EU country, got admitted as a lawyer there, and then repeated the manoeuvre in Germany.

"Helping people who really need this help motivates me a lot. People recognise my efforts and are very grateful," says Kühn. And her commitment to helping extends far beyond the professional sphere. She's just joined the Ricklingen District Council for the German Social Democratic Party (SPD) in Hanover South-West. In addition, she's a member of the 'Women Lawyers in the SPD' working group and is involved in an association that fights violence against women. "I have a lot of energy!" she laughs. And a husband who supports her: "My husband believes in me and supports me in everything I do." Her father provided the blueprint for her dedication to service: "He was also involved in social projects and wanted me to go into politics." In keeping with this wish, she had wanted to get involved in local politics in Rio, but wasn't elected at the time. In addition to her father, she cites Martin Luther King, Angela Merkel (for her assertiveness and calm demeanour), and Madonna (for her support of women's rights) as role models.

Kühn is proud that she never gave up and never let herself be deterred from her goals: "I don't care what other people say. However, I do listen to critics in order to improve myself." She's self-critical about not having given herself enough time to learn German: "If I'd started as soon as I first arrived in Germany, it would've been easier for my work." To her twelve-year-old self, looking for direction, she would counsel: "Believe in yourself, never give up – and study law."

Prof. Dr. Thomas Kapapa

NEUROCHIRURG

»Ich glaube daran, dass alles, was man braucht, in einem steckt.«

Bis heute kann Thomas Kapapa nicht sagen, wodurch er sich mehr stigmatisiert fühlt: seine Hautfarbe oder seine Behinderung. »Ich glaube, es ist eine Kombination aus beidem, die einige Menschen verunsichert und sie dann auf Distanz hält«, sagt er. Hautfarbe und Rollstuhl sind Äußerlichkeiten, aufgrund derer man Kapapa in eine Schublade stecken könnte. Sein Alter eignet sich ebenfalls dafür. Deswegen verrät er es nie. »Das gibt den Menschen nur eine weitere Information, mit der sie meinen, mich kategorisieren zu können«, sagt Kapapa. Nämlich als recht jungen, erfolgreichen Neurochirurgen. Denn Prof. Dr. Kapapa ist nicht nur Schwarz und körperlich eingeschränkt, sondern vor allem habilitierter Neurochirurg und Leitender Oberarzt am Universitätsklinikum Ulm. Und das aus eigener Kraft, trotz Behinderung und vieler Hindernisse – oder vielleicht genau deshalb.

Als zweites von fünf Kindern kommt Kapapa in Sambia zur Welt. Seine Eltern waren aus politischen Gründen aus ihrer Heimat Malawi in Südostafrika dorthin geflohen. Zuvor hatten sie sich bei ihrer medizinischen Ausbildung in Deutschland kennengelernt. Als Kapapa drei Jahre alt ist, siedelt die Familie wieder um: an die deutsche Nordseeküste, nach Emden in Ostfriesland. »Als Schwarze Familie in den 1980er-Jahren im Vorort einer Kleinstadt Anschluss zu finden, war gar nicht so einfach«, erinnert sich Kapapa. Doch die Familie bringt günstige Eigenschaften mit: Durchsetzungskraft, einen starken Willen und Bildung. Kapapas Vater ist vor Ort der einzige Arzt. Allein deswegen genießt er Respekt, Anerkennung und Autorität. Davon profitieren auch die Kinder, denn Vater Kapapa ist es, der dafür kämpft, dass sein Sohn auf eine Regelschule gehen kann, zu einer Zeit, in der Inklusion weder pädagogisch noch rein praktisch selbstverständlich ist. Doch Kapapa findet schnell gute Freunde. »Teilweise haben sie mich und meinen Rollstuhl die Treppen hochgetragen«, erinnert er sich.

Die Schulzeit ist für Kapapa eine extrem prägende Zeit. Da ist zum einen ein Mathelehrer, der ihn in der fünften Klasse furchtbar triezt. »Ich dachte, der mag mich nicht«, erzählt Kapapa. Bis der Lehrer ihn anspricht. »Du bist doch kein dummer Junge«, habe er damals zu ihm gesagt. Und: »Ich bin dafür da, um dein Potenzial aus dir herauszukitzeln.« Für diese Sätze ist Kapapa bis heute dankbar: Da ist einer, der ungemütlich wird, um ihn zu fordern. »Ich war nämlich extrem faul.« Und es zeigt dem Jugendlichen, dass er in der Lage ist, Dinge zu verändern und selbst etwas zu bewegen. Seiner Grundschullehrerin und zugleich Nachbarin sei er dankbar, weil sie die Familie bestärkt habe, ihn auf die Regelschule zu schicken. Und auch deren Tochter Conny. Sie ist Thomas' erste Freundin. »Sie hat mir das Selbstbewusstsein gegeben, dass man, auch wenn man im Rollstuhl sitzt, mit einem Mädchen zusammen sein kann«, sagt Kapapa voller Wärme.

NEUROSURGEON

"I believe that everything you need is inside of you."

To this day, Thomas Kapapa can't say what makes him feel more stigmatised: his skin colour or his disability. "I think it's a combination of the two that makes some people feel insecure and want to keep their distance," he says. Kapapa's skin colour and wheelchair use are just two aspects of his appearance that can lead to pigeonholing. His age also lends itself to this, which is why he never reveals it. "It just gives people another piece of information they think they can use to categorise me," explains Kapapa – namely, as a fairly young, successful neurosurgeon. Indeed, Professor Kapapa is not only a Black man with a disability, but also a PhD neurosurgeon and senior consultant at Ulm University Hospital. And he achieved this under his own steam, in spite of his disability and myriad obstacles – or perhaps precisely because of them.

Kapapa was born in Zambia, the second of five children. His parents had fled there from their home country of Malawi in Southeast Africa for political reasons, but originally met during their medical training in Germany. When Kapapa was three years old, the family moved again – this time to Emden in East Frisia on the German North Sea coast. "It wasn't easy for a Black family to make friends in the small-town suburbs of the 80s," Kapapa recalls. But the family arrived boasting certain desirable traits: perseverance, a strong will, and education. Kapapa's father was the only local doctor. For this reason, alone, he enjoyed respect, recognition and authority. The children also benefited from this; it was Kapapa's father who fought for his son to attend a mainstream school at a time when inclusion was not a given, whether for pedagogical or purely practical reasons. Nevertheless, Kapapa quickly made good friends. "Sometimes they carried me and my wheelchair up the stairs," he recalls.

School was a truly formative time for Kapapa. First, there was a teacher who bullied him horribly at the age of ten. "I thought he didn't like me," Kapapa says. That is, until the teacher told him: "You're not a stupid boy. It's my job to tease the potential out of you." Kapapa is still grateful for these words today because they showed this was a man willing to challenge him with a little tough love – "I was extremely lazy" – and it showed the boy that he was able to effect change and make a difference in the world. Likewise, he's grateful to his primary school teacher and neighbour, who encouraged the family to send him to a regular school. Gratitude is also owed to his teacher's daughter, Conny, Kapapa's first girlfriend. "She gave me the confidence of knowing that even if you're in a wheelchair, you can still be with a girl," Kapapa says warmly.

Und dann ist da noch sein Vater, der 2005 verstarb, der Mensch, über den Kapapa sagt, dass er ihn wohl am meisten geprägt habe. »Er hat mich behütet, gefordert und wichtige Lektionen gelehrt.« Etwa als Kapapa einen Unfall mit dem eigenen Auto hat, das er nur für den Schulweg nutzen soll. Der Unfall geschieht nicht auf dem Schulweg. Das Auto ist danach nicht mehr zu gebrauchen. »Da hat mein Vater gesagt, dass ich nun wohl wieder mit dem Bus fahren müsse, damit ich lerne, dass alles, was ich tue, Konsequenzen habe und ich für mein eigenes Handeln verantwortlich sei.« Auch dieser Satz stammt von ihm: »Lache niemals über jemanden, der rückwärtsläuft. Er könnte Anlauf nehmen.«

Die Berufswahl allerdings trifft er unabhängig vom Vater. »Ich habe auch mit Architektur und Jura geliebäugelt«, erzählt er. Doch die Juristerei ist ihm dann doch zu theoretisch. Von Architektur raten ihm Freunde ab. »Da musst du im Zweifel häufig auf Baustellen, das könnte schwierig

And then there's his father, who died in 2005 and was the person Kapapa says probably shaped him the most: "He protected me, challenged me and taught me important lessons." One example is the time when Kapapa had an accident in his car, which he was only supposed to use to get to school. The accident didn't happen on the way to school. Afterwards, the car had to be written off: "That's when my father said that I'd probably have to take the bus again now, so that I'd learn that everything I do has consequences and that I'm responsible for my own actions." The man was also famous for repeating the adage: "Never laugh at someone who's walking backwards. He might get off to a running start."

Nevertheless, Kapapa chose his career without his father's input. "I also had my eye on architecture and law," he explains. But law felt too theoretical for him. Meanwhile, friends advised him against

werden.« Also wird es die Medizin in Hannover. Und wieder sind es Freunde und Kollegen, die ihm Mut machen, gerade als er sich für das operative Fach der Neurochirurgie entscheidet. Auch später, als er sich an der Uni Ulm bewirbt, findet er in seinem Chef einen Menschen, der an ihn glaubt und ihm Dinge, die unmöglich oder zumindest schwierig scheinen, ermöglicht.

Doch bis dahin sei es ein langer Weg gewesen, auf dem er immer wieder gezweifelt und viel gelernt habe, auch über sich selbst. »Mein Vater würde als meine herausragende Charaktereigenschaft wohl Dickköpfigkeit nennen, im Laufe der Jahre ist aber Demut hinzugekommen, die ich mühsam erlernen musste«, sagt der nachdenkliche Mann. Demut für das Leben, das er führen kann, für die Menschen, die ihn unterstützen, allen voran seine Frau, und auch seinem Beruf gegenüber. »Wenn eine Behandlung mal nicht so erfolgreich war, stelle ich mir als Arzt immer die Frage, welchen Anteil mein Tun und ich selbst daran haben«, erklärt er. Das gelte auch für alle anderen Bereiche des Lebens. »Man darf Fehler machen, nur nicht zweimal unüberlegt den gleichen«, ist Kapapa überzeugt. »Ich halte es für sinnvoll, innezuhalten, wenn man nicht weiterweiß oder zweifelt.«

Er selbst bewundere mutige Menschen, die auf ihre Art ungehorsam seien. Ungehorsam dem gegenüber, was andere erwarten, so wie der englische Mittelstreckenläufer und spätere Neurologe Roger Bannister. Der lief 1956 als erster Mensch eine englische Meile in unter vier Minuten. »Dabei galt das damals als unmöglich, doch er hat es trotzdem gewagt«, sagt Kapapa voller Bewunderung. Oder der Basketballer Michael Jordan, der bei all seinen Erfolgen immer bescheiden geblieben sei, permanent an sich gearbeitet und nie lockergelassen habe. Und dann ist da noch Kapapas Idol aus der Kindheit: Captain Future, der Superheld und fähigste Wissenschaftler des Sonnensystems. »Er handelte immer überlegt und wusste, was er tat«, erklärt Kapapa seine kindliche Bewunderung von einst. Diese Eigenschaften habe auch er selbst entwickelt. »Ich halte mich für sehr überlegt und zugleich hitzköpfig, Freunde sprechen auch gern von meinem geradezu nervigen Optimismus.«

Dabei sei Kapapa manchmal selbst überrascht, was ihm alles gelungen sei und dass er trotz einiger Rückschläge niemals aufgegeben habe. »Die beiden wichtigsten Dinge in meinem Leben sind mein Beruf und die Liebe.« Beides sei für ihn nicht immer leicht miteinander zu vereinbaren. Denn Kapapas Job, den er als Passion bezeichnet, nimmt viel Zeit in Anspruch. »Manche nennen es auch Egoismus«, räumt er selbstkritisch ein. Dazu kommen seine Auszeiten auf seiner Terrasse, wo er jeden Sommer einen kleinen Dschungel anlegt, oder in der Autowerkstatt. Kapapa ist leidenschaftlicher Oldtimersammler und Bastler. Und einmal im Jahr fährt er nach Malawi, die Heimat seiner Eltern, auch um sein dortiges Projekt, den Aufbau einer neurochirurgischen Versorgung im Universitätskrankenhaus von Blantyre, voranzutreiben.

Kapapa ist dankbar für das Leben, das ihm möglich ist. Könnte er die Zeit zurückdrehen, würde er höchstens das Studium ein bisschen lockerer angehen, mehr Spaß haben. »Da war ich schon ganz schön verbissen«, sagt er im Rückblick. Seinem zwölfjährigen Ich würde er raten, »niemals Angst zu haben, denn irgendwann wird doch alles gut, wenn du selbst daran glaubst und arbeitest.« Er hat es schließlich weit gebracht als Schwarzer im Rollstuhl – vermeintliche Stigmata, die ihn inzwischen nicht mehr leiten.

architecture: "From time to time, you have to visit the construction site, which could be difficult." The young man therefore opted for medicine in Hanover. Once again, it was his friends and colleagues who encouraged him, especially when he decided to specialise in neurosurgery. Later, when he applied to the University of Ulm, he found himself working for a boss who believed in him and made things possible that had previously seemed impossible – or at least very difficult.

Nevertheless, it was a long road to that point in his career, which forced him to face his doubts time and again – and the young surgeon learnt a lot, including about himself. "My father would probably say that stubbornness is my biggest character trait, but over the years I've added some humility, which was hard for me to learn," says the thoughtful man. He therefore speaks modestly about the life he's able to lead, the people who support him – first and foremost, his wife – and even his profession. "If a treatment isn't successful, I always ask myself as a doctor what part I and my actions played in this," he explains. This also applies to all other areas of his life. "You can make mistakes, but you can't make the same mistake twice without thinking," Kapapa is convinced. "I think it makes sense to pause when you're stuck or unsure."

He admires courageous people who are disobedient in their own way, especially when it comes to meeting others' expectations – like the English middle-distance runner Roger Bannister, who went on to become a neurologist. In 1956, he was the first person to run an English mile in under four minutes. "At the time, that was considered impossible, but he dared to do it anyway," says Kapapa with admiration. Likewise, he looks up to basketball player Michael Jordan, who, despite all his successes, always stayed humble, constantly worked on improving himself, and never let up. And then there's Kapapa's childhood idol: Captain Future, a superhero and the most capable scientist in the solar system. "He always thought through his actions and knew what he was doing," states Kapapa, explaining his childhood fondness for the character. He says he went on to develop these qualities himself: "I consider myself very deliberate, but I can also be hot-tempered. And my friends say I'm downright annoyingly optimistic."

Kapapa is sometimes amazed at what he's been able to achieve – and that he's never given up despite a number of setbacks. "The two most important things in my life are love and my work." Yet the two have not always been easy bedfellows. This is because Kapapa's job, which he describes as a passion, takes up a lot of his time. "Some also call it self-centredness," he admits self-critically. Of course, he also enjoys downtime on his terrace, where he grows a mini jungle every summer, or at the car repair shop; Kapapa is a passionate collector and tinkerer of vintage cars. Once a year, he travels to his parents' homeland of Malawi to visit family and promote his local initiative: the establishment of neurosurgical care at the university hospital in Blantyre.

Kapapa is grateful for the life he's been able to lead. If he could turn back time, he would – at most – take a more relaxed approach to his studies and have a little more fun. "I was pretty single-minded back then," he says in retrospect. He'd advise his twelve-year-old self "never to be afraid because eventually everything will be alright if you believe in yourself and put in the work". After all, he's come a long way as a Black man in a wheelchair – supposed stigmas that no longer dictate the trajectory of his life today.

Arrey Kono Enow

MODEDESIGNERIN

»Ich glaube an die Kraft der Leidenschaft. Solange diese in dir brennt, kannst du alles erreichen.«

Arrey Kono Enow ist anders als andere Menschen: Als die Kinder in ihrem Alter mit Puppen spielen, schneidert die Vierjährige ihnen lieber Kleider aus abgetragenen Sachen, mit sieben will sie keine Sandalen mehr tragen, sondern Schuhe mit Absätzen. Als sie neun ist, geben ihre Eltern endlich nach. »Schon damals wusste ich, dass ich Modedesignerin werden wollte«, sagt sie. Als ihre Mitschülerinnen und Mitschüler unter der Strenge im Internat leiden, genießt sie die Freiheiten, die es ihr bietet. »Bei uns zu Hause ging es sehr viel strenger zu und im Internat konnte ich Regeln brechen und lernte gleichzeitig Disziplin.« Und als sie in Europa ist, in Italien lebt und für einen Besuch nach Deutschland kommt, empfindet sie die Menschen hier als viel offener und sympathischer als die im Land des Dolce Vita. »Ich mag Italien bis heute nicht besonders, obwohl mein Sohn dort lebt. Er ist ja sogar Italiener«, sagt sie. Arrey Kono Enow lässt sich nicht in Schubladen stecken, denkt nicht in solchen und sprengt sie selbst immer wieder. Ihren Kindheitstraum hat sie sich mit einem eigenen Modelabel, das sie in die ganze Welt verkauft, längst erfüllt.

Aufgewachsen in einer riesigen Familie mit drei leiblichen sowie zahlreichen Stief- und Halbgeschwistern, geht Arrey wie die meisten Kinder wohlhabender Eltern in Kamerun auf ein Internat. »Das war eine tolle Zeit, die dann aber auch irgendwann zu Ende war.« Zart hatte sie mal den Wunsch geäußert, nach Paris gehen zu wollen, um Mode zu studieren. »Da ist mein Vater, der Ingenieur war, durchgedreht, weil er Sorge hatte, dass ich Schneiderin werde, ich, seine Tochter, in deren Familie alle Akademiker sind«, erinnert sie sich und lacht dieses volle, kehlige Lachen, das sie als wichtigen Teil ihrer Persönlichkeit bezeichnet. Also überlegt sie sich etwas Bodenständigeres: Übersetzerin soll es sein. In Italien will sie die Ausbildung machen, um dann später nach Brüssel zu gehen. Doch es kommt anders. »Mir gefiel Italien nicht, die Ausbildung hat mich gelangweilt, wie mich überhaupt viele Dinge schnell langweilen.« Also nimmt sie sich eine Auszeit. In Rothenburg ob der Tauber verbessert sie ihr Deutsch. »Dort fand ich es toll, ich fand die Deutschen toll.« Sie bricht ihre Zelte in Italien ab und besucht das Goethe-Institut, dieses Mal in Prien am Chiemsee. Doch ihr Ziel heißt Berlin. Noch im selben Jahr, 1994, zieht sie von der bayerischen Provinz in die neue Hauptstadt Deutschlands. Befremden oder einen Kulturschock erlebt sie nicht. »Hier waren nur die Häuser höher, die Straßen sauberer und die Menschen weißer als bei uns in Kamerun«, sagt sie nüchtern.

In Berlin beginnt sie, Psychologie und Germanistik zu studieren, aber nichts davon führt sie zu Ende. Sie besucht die renommierte Modeschule ESMOD in Mailand, doch auch die bricht sie ab. »Ich hatte nicht das Gefühl, dass ich da wirklich etwas lerne«, sagt sie. An der Hochschule der Künste in Berlin wird sie abgelehnt. Doch Arrey Kono Enow weiß, dass Mode ihre Berufung ist, ihre Leidenschaft. Sie gibt nicht auf. Zu dieser

FASHION DESIGNER

"I believe in the power of passion. As long as it burns within you, you can achieve anything."

Arrey Kono Enow isn't like other people. While other four-year-olds played with dolls, she preferred to tailor outfits for them using old, worn-out clothes. At the age of seven, she no longer wanted to wear sandals, but shoes with heels. By the time she was nine, her parents finally gave in. "Even then, I knew I wanted to be a fashion designer," she says. While her classmates struggled with the strict atmosphere at boarding school, she enjoyed the freedom it offered her: "Things were much stricter at home, and at boarding school I could break the rules and learn self-discipline at the same time." When she came to live in Italy and travelled to Germany for a visit, she found the people there much friendlier and more open-minded than those in the home of the *dolce vita*. "I don't particularly like Italy to this day, even though my son lives there. He's even Italian!" she says. Enow doesn't allow herself to be pigeonholed, doesn't think in pigeonholes, and is always actively deconstructing them. She's long since fulfilled her childhood dream of creating her own fashion label and now it sells all over the world.

Enow grew up in a large family, boasting three biological siblings and countless step- and half-siblings. Like most children of wealthy parents, she was sent to boarding school in Cameroon: "It was a great time in my life, but it eventually came to an end." She once delicately expressed a desire to go to Paris to study fashion. "That's when my father, an engineer, went crazy because he was worried that I'd become a dressmaker – me, his daughter, in whose family everyone is an academic," she recalls, laughing that full, throaty laugh she describes as central to her identity. She therefore considered a more down-to-earth career: becoming a translator. She originally decided to qualify in Italy before moving on to Brussels, but that's not the way things turned out: "I didn't like Italy and my training bored me... so many things soon bore me." She therefore took some time out, seeking to improve her German in Rothenburg ob der Tauber: "I thought it was great there and I thought the Germans were great, too." She therefore broke camp in Italy and attended the Goethe Institute, this time in Prien am Chiemsee – but her final destination was Berlin. In the same year, 1994, she moved from the Bavarian provinces to Germany's new capital. In doing so, she experienced no sense of alienation or culture shock. "Here, the houses were simply taller, the streets were cleaner, and the people were whiter than in Cameroon," she says matter-of-factly.

In Berlin, she started programmes in psychology, German language, and literature, but she didn't finish any of them. She then attended the renowned ESMOD fashion school in Milan, but she dropped out of that too. "I didn't feel like I was really learning anything there," she explains. She was rejected by the Berlin University of the Arts.

Zeit finanziert sie ihr Leben sowieso schon, indem sie für Freunde näht, alles mit der Hand. Auch auf Flohmärkten verkauft sie ihre Stücke, doch das Geld reicht nicht. Dann beginnt sie, ihre Kleidungsstücke auch in Boutiquen anzubieten. »Aber ich wollte mein eigenes Label und meine eigene Herrin sein«, sagt sie. Knapp 3.000 Euro hat sie da gespart, dafür kauft sie Stoffe und lässt diese, wie sie es bis heute tut, plissieren. Auf dem Flohmarkt wird eine Frau auf ihre Entwürfe aufmerksam und bietet ihr an, sie zur Modemesse CPD nach Düsseldorf mitzunehmen. »Da hatte ich plötzlich einen Ministand und habe meine Kollektion innerhalb von drei Tagen an 42 Läden verkauft«, wundert sie sich heute noch ein bisschen und hat doch eine Erklärung dafür: »Die Leidenschaft stirbt nicht, das Feuer brennt immer bei mir«, sagt sie. Inzwischen hat sie längst einen eigenen Laden in den Hackeschen Höfen in Berlin, lebt von ihrer und für ihre Leidenschaft. Aufgeben gibt es für sie nicht, dafür immer Lösungen.

Daher bewundert Enow auch Frauen wie Kamala Harris, Angela Merkel und Hillary Clinton. »Diese Frauen lassen sich nicht von ihrem Weg abbringen, selbst wenn sie anecken oder sogar unbeliebt sind«, sagt sie. Jahrelang galt ihr auch Diana Ross als Vorbild. Aus einfachen Familienverhältnissen stammend, habe es die Sängerin zu Weltruhm gebracht, ohne sich beirren zu lassen. So lautet denn auch ihr Rat an alle Kinder und Jugendlichen: »Lass dir niemals einreden, dass andere besser sind als du. Hör am besten einfach nicht hin.« Dies habe sie schon von klein auf gewusst, auch wenn es nicht immer einfach gewesen sei. Die Modedesignerin bilanziert: »Wer eine dunkle Hautfarbe hat, muss doppelt so viel Leistung zeigen, um Erfolg zu haben, wie Menschen mit weißer Hautfarbe.«

Eine dunkle Hautfarbe bedeutet für sie aber vor allem enorme Schönheit – eine Einstellung, die sie auch ihrer Stiefmutter zu verdanken habe, sagt sie. Jener Frau, die immer sehr auf ihr Äußeres bedacht gewesen sei, sich stets elegant gekleidet und den Kindern vor allem eine wichtige Botschaft mit auf den Weg gegeben habe: »Bevor ihr heiratet, müsst ihr so viel Spaß haben wie möglich und vor allem dafür sorgen, dass ihr eure Rechnungen selber bezahlen könnt.« Spaß hat Enow bis heute und ihre Rechnungen zahlt sie sowieso selbst.

Die Wahlberlinerin, die ihr Geburtsjahr nicht verrät – »Das Alter ist in Afrika nicht wichtig« –, ist ohnehin stolz, ja dankbar für ihre Herkunft. »Ich hätte auch in einem anderen Land geboren werden können, in eine andere Familie hinein«, sagt sie. Ihr aber seien viele Geschenke in die Wiege gelegt worden, vor allem ihre Kreativität, die sie erkannt habe und von der sie leben könne. Und dann sei da noch die große Liebe, die sie empfange und in sich trage. »Dafür bin ich dankbar, und stolz bin ich auf meinen Sohn, der ein so toller Mensch geworden ist, trotz der schrägen Mami.« Schräg – und außergewöhnlich!

Nevertheless, Enow knew that fashion was her passion and vocation, and she wouldn't give up. By this time, she was earning a living by hand-sewing items for friends. She also sold her pieces at flea markets, but the money wasn't enough to get by on. Then, she started offering her garments in boutiques as well. "But I wanted to have my own label and be my own boss," she says. Enow worked to save just under €3,000, which she used to buy fabrics and have them pleated, as she still does today. At one flea market, a woman noticed her designs and offered to take her to the CPD fashion fair in Düsseldorf. "Suddenly, I had a mini stand and sold my collection to 42 shops within three days," she says, still marvelling at this turn of events today... yet she also has an explanation for it: "My passion never died; that fire was still burning inside me." Since then, Enow has acquired her own shop in the Hackesche Höfe in Berlin, where she lives off and for her passion. For her, there's no such thing as giving up. There are *always* solutions.

This is one reason Enow admires women like Kamala Harris, Angela Merkel and Hillary Clinton. "These women never let themselves be swayed from their paths, even if they're controversial or unpopular," she explains. For years, another of her role models was Diana Ross. Rising from humble beginnings, the singer never faltered in pursuing global fame. Enow's advice to all children and young people is: "Never let anyone tell you that others are better than you. It's best just not to listen." This is a tip she picked up at an early age, even if it wasn't always easy to take to heart. The fashion designer can sum up her experiences in a single sentence: "If you have darker skin, you have to perform twice as well as someone white to be successful."

Nevertheless, she thinks dark skin is incredibly beautiful – an attitude she owes, in part, to her step-mother. This woman, who always took great pride in her appearance and never failed to dress elegantly, taught her children one important lesson: "Before you get married, you have to have as much fun as possible and, above all, make sure you can pay your own bills." Enow is still having fun today and naturally pays her own way in life.

The adoptive Berlin resident, who chooses not to reveal her year of birth – "Age is not important in Africa" – is proud, nay grateful, for her origins. "I could have been born in another country and into another family," she says. Yet she was born with many gifts – not least her creativity, which she recognised and which allows her to earn a living today. And then there's the great love she carries with her through life: "For that I'm grateful, and I'm proud of my son, who's become such a great person, despite having a slightly kooky mummy!" Kooky, perhaps, but undeniably extraordinary!

Dr. Akuma Saningong

NATURWISSENSCHAFTLER, PERSÖNLICHKEITSCOACH, KEYNOTE UND MOTIVATIONAL SPEAKER

»Ich glaube an die Kraft der Emotionen, die uns in Bewegung hält und zu allem befähigt, an das wir glauben.«

Akuma Saningong ist mit Witzen über Deutsche aufgewachsen – und mit deutschen Schimpfwörtern. »Kruzifix«, entfuhr es seiner Großmutter immer, wenn sie sich über etwas ärgerte oder wenn der kleine Akuma oder seine sechs Geschwister mal wieder etwas ausgefressen hatten. Sie selbst hatte die Flüche von ihrer Großmutter gelernt, die die deutsche Kolonialherrschaft in Kamerun noch erlebt hatte. Vielleicht lag es an diesen frühen Berührungspunkten, dass sich Saningong noch während seines Chemiestudiums in Jaunde dazu entschloss, nach Deutschland zu gehen. »Ich wollte mehr von der Welt sehen und neben unseren Landessprachen Englisch und Französisch eine weitere Sprache lernen«, erzählt er. Es hätte auch Spanien oder Italien werden können, es wurde aber Deutschland. Das war im Jahr 2001.

Den Auslandsaufenthalt ermöglichen ihm seine Eltern, der Vater Anwalt, die Mutter Angestellte. Wie seine Geschwister hatte er vorher ein Internat besucht – in dem zentralafrikanischen Land die Voraussetzung für eine gute Bildung. »Dafür bin ich meinen Eltern sehr dankbar«, sagt Saningong. Die Familie sei nicht reich gewesen, als gut bürgerlich würde er sie bezeichnen. Für Internate und ein Studium für alle sieben Kinder habe es gereicht.

Noch in Kamerun besucht der 1978 geborene Saningong das Goethe-Institut. Gute Deutschkenntnisse sind damals wie heute die Voraussetzung, um ein Visum für ein Studium in Deutschland zu bekommen. Der ehrgeizige junge Mann entscheidet sich für Biotechnologie in Darmstadt. »Das war ein zukunftsorientierter Studiengang mit guten Jobaussichten.« Das ist ihm wichtig. Es folgt die Promotion an der Universität Duisburg-Essen. Als er anschließend als Unternehmensberater arbeitet, zweifelt er erstmals an seiner Jobentscheidung. »Die Arbeit war abwechslungsreich, wurde gut bezahlt, aber sie hat mich nicht ausgefüllt«, erinnert sich Saningong. Ihm fehlen bei der Arbeit die emotionalen Aspekte, eine gewisse Spiritualität, die in Entscheidungen bei den Kunden mit einfließen. Etwa zeitgleich lernt er die Lehren des US-amerikanischen Zellbiologen Dr. Bruce H. Lipton, des US-amerikanischen Neurowissenschaftlers Dr. Joe Dispenza und des indisch-US-amerikanischen Quantenphysikers Dr. Amit Goswami kennen. Sie alle verbinden Naturwissenschaften mit Persönlichkeitsentwicklung. Für Saningong werden sie zu Vorbildern, zu spirituellen Mentoren.

Saningong ist überzeugt, dass in jedem ein riesiges Potenzial steckt, viele es nur nicht kennen. Bei genau dieser Persönlichkeitsentwicklung hilft er Menschen als Motivationsexperte und Persönlichkeitscoach sowie als Keynote Speaker auf der ganzen Welt. »Unsere Gesellschaft ist sehr kopforientiert, möchte Entscheidungen mit Fakten untermauert haben«, begründet der promovierte Biotechnologe seine Meinung.

SCIENTIST, LIFE COACH, KEYNOTE SPEAKER AND MOTIVATIONAL SPEAKER

"I believe in the power of emotions to keep us moving and enable us to achieve whatever we set our minds to."

Born in 1978, Akuma Saningong grew up with jokes about Germans – and with German swear words. *"Kruzifix!"* was a common refrain when his grandmother was angry or when little Saningong or one of his six siblings had got up to mischief. She, in turn, had learnt the phrases from her own grandmother, who had lived through German colonial rule in Cameroon. Perhaps it was because of this early exposure to German culture that Saningong decided to move to Germany while studying chemistry in Yaoundé: "I wanted to see more of the world and learn another language alongside our national languages, English and French." He could have picked Spain or Italy, but Germany was his choice. And that was back in 2001.

His move abroad was made possible by his parents, his father being a lawyer and his mother being an office worker. Like his siblings, he'd previously attended a boarding school – a prerequisite for a good education in his Central African country. "I'm very grateful to my parents for that," Saningong says. His family was not rich; Saningong would describe them as middle-class – yet this was enough to ensure a place at boarding school and degrees for all seven children.

While still in Cameroon, Saningong attended the Goethe Institute because (just like today) a good knowledge of German was a prerequisite for obtaining a visa to study in Germany. The ambitious scholar ultimately decided to study biotechnology in Darmstadt; it was a "future-oriented degree with good job prospects", something important to him. He followed his degree with a PhD at the University of Duisburg-Essen. When he subsequently began work as a management consultant, he found himself doubting his career decisions for the first time. "The work was varied and paid well, but it didn't really satisfy me," Saningong recalls. He felt the work lacked an emotional aspect – a certain spirituality that flows into client decision-making. Around the same time, he became acquainted with the teachings of American cell biologist Dr Bruce H. Lipton, American neuroscientist Dr Joe Dispenza and Indian-American quantum physicist Dr Amit Goswami, all of whom combine the natural sciences with personal development. For Saningong, they became role models and spiritual mentors.

Saningong is convinced that everyone has great potential, but many just don't know it. And it's with precisely this that he wishes to help people around the world in his role as an expert life coach, keynote speaker and motivational speaker. "Our society is very logic-oriented and we want our decisions to be backed up by facts," argues the PhD biotechnologist. And he knows that many reactions, decisions and emotions can be explained biochemically. Take laughter, for

Und er weiß, dass viele Reaktionen, Entscheidungen und Gefühlsregungen biochemisch zu erklären sind. Das Lachen zum Beispiel. Der Mann, der selbst gern und viel lacht, sagt: »Jedes Lächeln bringt mich zum Lachen, allerdings nicht nur, weil ein lächelndes Gegenüber in meinem Gehirn biochemische Reaktionen auslöst.« Lachen ist für ihn auch Ausdruck eines positiven Lebensgefühls, von Offenheit und Zugewandtheit.

Einfach sind die Anfänge als selbstständiger Coach nicht. »Natürlich hat man Angst, dass man es nicht schafft, dass das Geld nicht für die Miete reicht«, erinnert er sich. Kundenkontakte aufzubauen, ist anstrengend und herausfordernd, sich einen Namen zu machen auch. Doch er arrangiert sich mit den Ungewissheiten und der Unsicherheit, die eine Selbstständigkeit mit sich bringt. »Man kann das nur aushalten, wenn man davon überzeugt ist, was man tut«, sagt er und führt ein Zitat von Friedrich Nietzsche an: »Wer das Warum kennt, dem ist kein Wie zu schwer«, heißt es in einer leicht abgewandelten Fassung.

Saningong will seine Geschichte mit anderen teilen und etwas weitergeben, um andere Menschen zu ermutigen. Er sei dankbar für das, was er bislang erlebt und welchen Weg sein Leben genommen habe. Zu einem seiner wichtigsten Unterstützer wird noch während des Studiums Helmut Lotz. Er ist einer der Alten Herren der Katholischen Deutschen Studentenverbindung Nassovia zu Darmstadt, der Saningong beitritt. Lotz gewährt dem jungen Afrikaner ein Stipendium. »Er hat mich gelehrt, was Geben bedeutet und dass Hilfe keine Grenzen kennt, keine familiären, keine gesellschaftlichen, religiösen oder ethnischen«, sagt Saningong. Bereits 2007 gründet er selbst den gemeinnützigen Verein Kamerun4AfrikaClub e. V. (KAC e. V.), der Bildungsstipendien an Kinder und Jugendliche in Afrika vergibt. Um sein soziales Engagement auszuweiten, das auf Spenden angewiesen ist, gründet der inzwischen in Hamburg lebende Saningong die KAC-Afrika GmbH, ein Unternehmen, das afrikanische und deutsche Unternehmen zusammenbringt, Technologie, Forschung und Bildung fördert.

Für Saningong hat sein Engagement etwas mit Dankbarkeit und Demut zu tun, den beiden für ihn wohl wichtigsten Eigenschaften. »Wer demütig ist, sieht andere, kann sein Ego herunterschrauben, um mit anderen auf eine Augenhöhe zu gelangen«, sagt er und räumt ein, dass auch ihm das nicht immer leichtgefallen sei. Er selbst könne impulsiv sein und seine Überzeugungen durchdrücken, wenn er dahinterstehe. Auch diese Charakterzüge hätten ihn wohl dahin gebracht, wo er heute stehe. Doch auch wenn er im Laufe seines Lebens gelernt habe, sich selbst zurückzunehmen – mit Schwäche oder Unterwürfigkeit habe das nichts zu tun, sondern eben mit Stärke, Achtsamkeit und Respekt, sich selbst und anderen Menschen gegenüber.

Daher hält Saningong auch nichts von dem Begriff »Held« oder »Stolz«. »Für mich ist jeder Mensch ein Held, weil er etwas weiß oder kann, das ich nicht weiß oder kann«, sagt er. Helden würden schnell auf ein unerreichbares Podest gestellt. Saningong ist aber überzeugt, dass jeder Mensch alles erreichen kann, was er wirklich will. Die Kreativität und die menschlichen Möglichkeiten, die jeder in sich trage, überraschten ihn immer wieder. »Es gibt immer eine Lösung für Probleme, und wenn es mehrere zu geben scheint, sollte man die Gedanken darüber sacken lassen. Dann kristallisiert sich die richtige Lösung heraus«, ist er überzeugt. Stolz hingegen könne sich schnell in Arroganz oder Überheblichkeit verwandeln.

Wichtig ist Saningong, dass jeder bei sich selbst beginnt, um mit der Welt und anderen Menschen im Einklang zu leben – auch in Bezug auf

example. The scientist, who loves to laugh, says: "Every smile makes me laugh, but not just because smiling triggers biochemical reactions in my brain." For him, laughter is also an expression of a positive attitude to life, openness and friendliness.

Starting out as a self-employed coach isn't easy. "Of course, you're afraid you won't make it and that the money won't be enough to pay the rent," he recalls. Building client lists is a demanding challenge, and so is making a name for yourself, but he's come to terms with the uncertainties and insecurity that come with being your own boss. "You can only endure it if you're utterly convinced of what you're doing," he says, citing a slightly modified quote by Friedrich Nietzsche: "No how is too difficult for those who know the why."

Saningong wants to share his story and pass on something to encourage others. He's grateful for what he's experienced so far and for the path his life has taken. Helmut Lotz became one of the coach's most important supporters while he was still a student. He was one of the old guard at the Darmstadt Catholic German Student Association, Nassovia, which Saningong joined. Lotz gifted the young African student a scholarship. "He taught me what giving means and that help knows no bounds, whether familial, social, religious or ethnic," says Saningong. Later, in 2007, Saningong, founded his own non-profit association, Kamerun4AfrikaClub e.V. (KAC e.V.), which grants scholarships to children and young people in Africa. In order to expand his charitable activities, which rely on donations, Saningong – who now lives in Hamburg – also founded KAC-Afrika GmbH, a company that brings together African and German companies to promote technology, research and education.

His activism goes hand in hand with gratitude and humility, probably the two most important qualities to him. "If you're humble, you can see others; you can lower your ego and see eye to eye with other people," he says, admitting that this has not always been easy for him. He explains that he can be impulsive and assert his beliefs a little too forcefully at times. Yet these are probably also the traits that have got him to where he is today. While he's learnt to take a step back in life, this has nothing to do with weakness or submissiveness, but rather with strength, attentiveness and respect for himself and others.

That's why Saningong doesn't think much of words like 'hero' or 'pride'. "To me, everyone's a hero because they know or can do something I don't or can't," he says. He believes that heroes are quickly placed on an unattainable pedestal. Nevertheless, he remains convinced that anyone can achieve anything they truly want. Saningong also admits that the creativity and human potential everyone has within them never ceases to surprise him. "There's always a solution to problems, and when there seems to be more than one, you should let your thoughts around the problem settle. The right solution will soon become clear," he asserts. Pride, on the other hand, can quickly turn into arrogance and hubris.

Saningong believes that living in harmony with the world and its people must start with oneself – and this also applies to your skin colour. "When I first came to Europe and found myself on a small plane travelling from Switzerland to Germany, I was the only Black person and felt like everyone was watching me, but that wasn't the case at all," he recalls. He learnt from this experience that "you see

die eigene Hautfarbe. »Als ich nach Europa kam und irgendwann in einem kleinen Flugzeug von der Schweiz nach Deutschland saß, war ich der einzige Schwarze und fühlte mich von allen beobachtet, doch dem war gar nicht so«, erinnert er sich. Er habe daraus gelernt, »dass man in anderen sieht, was man selbst glaubt«, und das gelte es zu hinterfragen. So hält er es auch mit Rassismus. »Ich habe ihn einfach aus meinem Kopf gestrichen, sehe keine unterschiedlichen Hautfarben mehr«, sagt er. Zugleich ist er vorsichtig optimistisch, was Diskriminierung angeht, die es seiner Meinung nach in jeder Gesellschaft gibt. »Rassismus ist gelernt, egal ob er institutionell oder individuell ist, daher kann man ihn auch verlernen oder abtrainieren«, sagt er, und da kommt wieder der Naturwissenschaftler in ihm zum Vorschein.

Daher lautet auch sein Rat an sein zwölfjähriges Ich nach einer buddhistischen Weisheit, stets offen zu sein und sich an nichts zu binden. »Halte dir alle Optionen offen, sage nicht schnell Ja oder Nein, sondern hör zu und gib den Dingen etwas Zeit, damit sie klarer werden.« Die richtigen Antworten kämen dann wie von selbst. Denn Saningong ist überzeugt: »Emotionen sind Energie in Bewegung.« Daraus gelte es zu schöpfen.

in others what you believe yourself", and that's what needs to be questioned. He feels the same way about racism. "I just put that out of my mind and I don't see the different skin colours anymore," he says. At the same time, he's cautiously optimistic about discrimination, which he believes exists in every society. "Racism is learnt, whether it's institutional or individual, so it can be unlearnt or trained out of a person," he says. This is where the naturalist in him resurfaces.

Reflecting on Buddhist wisdom, his advice to his twelve-year-old self would be to always stay open and not to commit to anything: "Keep all your options open. Don't be too quick to say yes or no, but listen and give things some time to crystallise." That way, the right answers will naturally present themselves. Saningong is convinced that "emotions are energy in motion" – and that this is a notion we should all tap into.

Vivian Abena Ansuhenne

HEILPRAKTIKERIN

»Ich glaube an mich, daran, auf mich selbst zu hören und mir zu vertrauen.«

Vivian Abena Ansuhenne ist sich schon früh sicher: »Durch mich wirkt eine Kraft.« Dieser Erkenntnis folgend, zeichnet sich bald ihr Wunsch ab, Menschen behandeln zu wollen. Als Heilpraktikerin mit eigener Praxis folgt sie ihrer Bestimmung.

Die Tochter ghanaischer Eltern, Jahrgang 1972, wächst mit zwei Brüdern im Haushalt ihres Vaters auf, nachdem sich die Eltern getrennt haben. »Ich hatte eine tolle Kindheit in Geesthacht, bin gern zur Schule gegangen.« Sechs Wochen Sommerferien seien immer zu lang gewesen. »Für die Menschen, die meine Kindheit geprägt haben, Freundinnen und Freunde, Menschen aus meiner Nachbarschaft, bin ich sehr dankbar. Besonders meine Eltern sind meine Vorbilder.« Ihre Hartnäckigkeit und das Festhalten an Zielen habe sie von ihrer Mutter geerbt, einer medizinisch-technischen Assistentin und Hausfrau. Schon die habe sich gern weitergebildet, und auch den Vater, einen Chirurgen, erinnere sie zu Hause immer über Fachbüchern gebeugt. Beide hätten ihr den Freiraum gegeben, den sie gebraucht habe, um sich zu entwickeln. Die Trennung der Eltern sei für sie wie aus heiterem Himmel gekommen, zumal sie von etwaigen vorausgegangenen Streitereien nichts mitbekommen habe. Bei der Zwölfjährigen löst die Trennung aus, dass sie schnell sehr verantwortungsbewusst wird.

Freundinnen spielen in ihrem Leben schon früh eine bedeutende Rolle. »Es war ein männlicher Haushalt, in dem ich aufgewachsen bin, und deshalb habe ich mir unbewusst sehr feminine Freundinnen gesucht, mit denen ich meine Weiblichkeit ausleben konnte«, lautet ihre Erklärung. Sie habe sehr auf schöne Kleidung und ein gepflegtes Aussehen geachtet. In diese Phase fällt auch ihr erster Berufswunsch, Stewardess zu werden.

Ein tragisches Ereignis bewirkt ein Umdenken und eine neue Standortbestimmung in ihrem Leben. Im Alter von 25 Jahren stirbt ihr jüngerer Bruder bei einem tragischen Unfall. »Das hat mich sehr geprägt. Vorher habe ich viel Party gemacht, doch plötzlich fand ich alles oberflächlich.« So wendet sie sich von einem Teil ihres Freundeskreises ab. Im Laufe der Zeit findet sie jedoch wieder die Balance aus hintergründigen Gesprächen und ausgelassenem Zusammensein mit alten und neuen Freunden.

Frauen mit einer selbstbewussten Ausstrahlung findet Ansuhenne bewundernswert, doch Heldenstatus erreicht bei ihr niemand. »Dazu sehe ich die Menschen zu ganzheitlich, viel zu menschlich.« Angesichts dieses umfassenden Blicks auf die menschliche Spezies wähnt man sich als Patientin oder Patient bei ihr in guten Händen. 1999 beginnt sie zu praktizieren, ab 2017 als alleinige Inhaberin einer Praxis, zuvor mit Anmietungen eines Raumes und Teilhabe an Gemeinschaftspraxen. Betrachtet man ihre Vita, so hat sie sich pausenlos fortgebildet. Die Liste der Kurse, die sie seit ihrer zweijährigen Heilpraktikerausbildung und der direkt daran anschließenden dreijährigen Ausbildung im Bereich Traditionelle Chinesische Medizin (TCM) besucht hat, ist umfassend. Unter anderem bildet sich Ansuhenne in Dermatologie sowie kosmetischer Akupunktur

ALTERNATIVE MEDICAL PRACTITIONER

"I believe in myself, in listening to myself, and in trusting myself."

Vivian Abena Ansuhenne felt it from an early age: "A power is working through me." After gaining this insight, she soon understood that she wanted to treat others. As an alternative medical practitioner with her own practice, she's now following her destiny.

Born in Germany in 1972 to Ghanaian parents, Ansuhenne grew up with her two brothers in her father's home after her parents' divorce. For her, six weeks of summer holidays was always too long: "I had a wonderful childhood in Geesthacht and loved going to school. I'm very grateful for the people who shaped my childhood, including my friends and people in the local community. My parents are my greatest role models." She got her tenacity and perseverance in pursuing her goals from her mother, a medico-technical assistant and house wife who never stopped educating herself. Vivian remembers her father, a surgeon, was also always hunched over reference books at home. Both parents gave her the freedom she needed to flourish. Her parents' separation came like a bolt from the blue, especially since she'd not been aware of any quarrelling, causing the twelve-year-old to quickly develop a strong sense of responsibility.

Her friends played an important role in her life from an early age: "I grew up in a very masculine household, so I unconsciously sought out very girly friends who could help me to express my femininity," she explains. She was especially drawn to beautiful clothes and a well-groomed appearance. At this stage in her life, her first career aspiration was to become a flight attendant.

Then, a shocking event prompted a rethink and a new direction for her in life. At the age of 25, her younger brother died in a tragic accident: "That had a big impact on me. Before then, I partied a lot, but suddenly I found it all very superficial." The experience caused her to turn her back on certain friendships. However, over time, she once again found a way to balance deep conversations and boisterous get-togethers with old and new friends, alike.

Ansuhenne finds women with a self-confident aura admirable, but no one achieves hero status with her: "I see people too holistically, far too humanly, for that." It's thanks to this all-encompassing view of the human condition that Ansuhenne's patients always feel they're in good hands. She became an alternative medical practitioner in 1999 and has run her own practice since 2017, having previously rented spaces in group practices. Looking at her CV, it's clear that she's never stopped learning; she's taken a litany of courses since completing two years of training in alternative medicine and three years of training in traditional Chinese medicine (TCM). Among other things, Ansuhenne is currently continuing her education in dermatology and cosmetic acupuncture, and is working to complete 200 hours of intensive training to become a yoga instructor. "I like to learn!" she says of her marathon education. She also enjoys

weiter und absolviert eine 200-stündige Intensivausbildung zur Yogalehrerin. »Ich mag es, mich fortzubilden«, lautet ihr schlichter Kommentar zum Bildungsmarathon. Das Erlernte gibt sie gern weiter, unter anderem von 2013 bis 2019 als Dozentin für Akupunktur und TCM an einem Hamburger TCM-Institut, an dem sie viele Jahre zuvor selbst ihr Wissen erworben hat. »Ich bin fasziniert von TCM, finde die Heilkunst toll und kreativ, auch die Denkweise.«

Sowohl in Bezug auf ihr berufliches als auch ihr privates Leben würde sie alles noch einmal genauso entscheiden, wie sie es getan hat, würde nichts ändern wollen, wenn sie denn jemals die Chance dazu hätte. Diese tiefe Zufriedenheit mit ihrem bisherigen Lebensweg komme daher, so die auf Hauterkrankungen und Allergien spezialisierte Heilpraktikerin, dass sie vor allen anstehenden Entscheidungen nachdenken würde, niemals spontan entscheide. Ein-, zweimal habe sie auf den Rat von Freunden gehört und es später bereut. Während viele andere Menschen die Sicherheit benötigten, einen Plan B in der Tasche zu haben, sagt Ansuhenne: »Ich stelle mir vor, wie ich leben möchte, und tue so lange etwas, bis Plan A funktioniert. Ich bin eher abenteuerlustig.«

Bei so viel Zielstrebigkeit und beruflichem Ehrgeiz ist es nicht erstaunlich, dass die Heilpraktikerin direkt nach der Ausbildung zur pharmazeutisch-technischen Assistentin (PTA) die nächste Ausbildung in Angriff nimmt. Auslöser ist ein Artikel in einer Zeitschrift über den Beruf der Heilpraktikerin. »Ich kannte den Beruf vorher gar nicht«, so Ansuhenne. Zu diesem Zeitpunkt plant sie eigentlich, nach der PTA-Ausbildung ihren Lebensunterhalt als Pharmareferentin zu bestreiten. Doch der Bericht hinterlässt nachhaltigen Eindruck, und Ansuhenne beginnt direkt nach Abschluss ihrer Prüfung mit der schulischen Heilpraktikerausbildung.

Ihre Arbeit als Dozentin, Kreateurin von TCM-Mischungen aus chinesischen Heilpflanzen und Vitalpilzen, Organisatorin von Fachseminaren, Onlinekursen und -vorträgen zu Themen wie Gesundheitsbewusstsein und Anti-Aging sieht die Freiberuflerin als Ausläufer ihrer Kreativität. »Ich bin so froh, dass ich immer den Weg gegangen bin, den ich gehen wollte – ganz gleich, wie holprig er war.« Ihrem zwölfjährigen Ich würde Ansuhenne zuflüstern, ganz ruhig zu bleiben und auf das zu hören, was ihre innere Stimme sagt. »Vertraue ihr.« Wenn sich Fehler einstellten, sich sogar wiederholten, könne man an sich arbeiten. »Ich sehe Fehler nicht als etwas Schlimmes, sondern vielmehr als Hinweis darauf, etwas zu verbessern.« Über sich selbst könne sie auch sehr gut lachen. Genauer: über die Gedanken, die ihr kämen, und auch über manche Entscheidungen, die sie getroffen habe.

Ihre Hautfarbe verbindet Ansuhenne damit, dass sie ursprünglich aus Ghana kommt. »Die ist und war für mich nie relevant.« Nichtsdestotrotz findet sie Gefallen daran und sagt: »Ich hatte nie das Bedürfnis, anders zu sein.« Jemand, der eine andere Person wegen ihrer Hautfarbe nicht akzeptieren kann, wie sie ist, ist ihrer Meinung nach ein Rassist. Rassismus sei ein anderes Wort für Intoleranz und Inakzeptanz, eine begrenzte Denkweise, unabhängig von der Hautfarbe. Sie selbst erinnert sich nicht daran, beim Aufwachsen in Geesthacht mit rassistischen Denkweisen konfrontiert worden zu sein. Trotz Höhen und Tiefen in ihrem Berufsleben als Heilpraktikerin habe es nie den Moment gegeben, an dem sie aufhören wollte. Sie sei manchmal selbst überrascht, dass sie in allen Dingen etwas Positives sehe und sich selbst immer wieder gut motivieren könne. Dabei sei es nicht relevant, ob etwas anstrengend sei oder nicht. Das Kraftreservoir von Vivian Abena Ansuhenne, so hat es den Anschein, ist unerschöpflich.

passing on what she's learnt, having even spent a six-year stint from 2013 to 2019 as a lecturer in acupuncture and TCM at Hamburg the TCM institute, where she, herself, learnt her craft many years earlier: "I'm fascinated by TCM. I find the art of healing – and the associated mindset – wonderfully creative."

Looking back on her personal and professional life, she'd make all the same choices again; if given the chance to start over, she wouldn't want to change a thing. The alternative medical practitioner, who specialises in skin diseases and allergies, maintains that this deep satisfaction with her life so far stems from the fact that she always thinks before making any decisions; nothing is ever decided spontaneously. Once or twice, she's listened to the advice of friends and later come to regret it. While many other people need the security of having a Plan B, Ansuhenne says, "I imagine how I want to live and keep plugging away until Plan A works. I'm an adventurous sort."

Given the extent of her determination and professional ambition, it's not surprising that Ansuhenne started her next training course immediately after qualifying as a pharmaceutical technical assistant (PTA). The trigger was a magazine article about the alternative medical profession. "I'd never heard of the profession before then," Ansuhenne says. At the time, she was actually planning to make a living as a pharmaceutical sales representative after completing her PTA training. However, the article made a lasting impression and Ansuhenne applied herself to the theory of alternative medicine immediately after completing her final exams.

The freelancer would describe her work – as a lecturer, creator of TCM mixtures from Chinese medicinal plants and vital mushrooms, and organiser of specialist seminars, online courses and lectures on topics like health awareness and anti-aging – as an offshoot of her creativity: "I'm so glad that I always went the way I wanted to go no matter how bumpy the road was." Ansuhenne would whisper to her twelve-year-old self to stay very calm and listen to what her inner voice is saying: "Trust it." She counsels that if mistakes happen, even repeatedly, you can always work on yourself: "I don't see mistakes as something bad, but rather as an indication of where we can improve." She's also very good at laughing at herself – or, more precisely, at some of the thoughts she's had and some of the decisions she's made.

Ansuhenne associates her skin colour with the fact that she originally comes from Ghana: "It's not and never has been relevant to me." Nevertheless, she likes it: "I never felt the need to be different." Someone who can't accept another person as they are because of their skin colour is a racist, in her opinion. And racism, she says, is another word for intolerance and unacceptance – a limited way of thinking, regardless of skin colour. She doesn't recall being confronted with racist attitudes while growing up in Geesthacht. Despite the ups and downs in her career as an alternative medical practitioner, she says there was never a moment when she wanted to quit. She's sometimes surprised that she finds a silver lining in every situation and can always motivate herself, no matter how arduous the task before her. It would seem that Vivian Abena Ansuhenne's well of strength is inexhaustible.

Anthony Sarpong

STERNEKOCH

»Ich glaube an die Würde eines jeden Menschen. Wer die respektiert, wird selbst zu einem glücklichen Menschen.«

Anthony Sarpong hat seinen Eltern viele Eigenschaften zu verdanken, die ihn zu dem Mann gemacht haben, der er heute ist. Das Motto seines Vaters lautet: »Leben und leben lassen.« Das lehrte Sarpong Toleranz und Selbstbewusstsein. Seine Mutter brachte ihm die Kunst des Kochens näher. »Bei uns in Ghana ist Kochen ein Stück Kultur. Da wird gesungen, getanzt. Die Lebensfreude, die damit verbunden ist, ist unfassbar«, sagt er. Sarpong ist Sternekoch mit eigenem Restaurant im niederrheinischen Meerbusch, Vater von drei Kindern, begeisterter Sportler – ein Mann, der glücklich ist und fast alles erreicht hat, was er sich wünschte. Und der dabei »tiefenentspannt« ist. Das sagt der 1982 in Ghana geborene Sarpong nicht nur von sich selbst, das spürt jeder, der ihm begegnet. Liebe habe er von Vater wie Mutter gleichermaßen erfahren. Und so ist Anthony Sarpong ein Mensch, der von innen heraus strahlt und diese Wärme, Freundlichkeit und Ausgeglichenheit an andere weitergibt.

Ende der 1980er-Jahre entscheidet sich Sarpongs Familie dafür, nach Deutschland zu gehen. »Meinem Papa war es wichtig, dass wir etwas lernen, und zwar im Ausland«, erzählt der Unternehmer. Denn, so ist der Vater überzeugt, nur wer außerhalb Afrikas ausgebildet wird, kann in der Welt Anerkennung erlangen. Also geht die damals vierköpfige Familie nach Wiesbaden, der Vater arbeitet auf der Air Base. Anthony kommt direkt in die erste Klasse, mit nur einigen Brocken Deutsch. Er ist der einzige Schwarze damals, doch das stört ihn nicht. Er weiß sich zu wehren, auch schon mal mit Fäusten. Heute hat er eine andere Strategie.

Schon als kleiner Junge ist er kreativ, hibbelig und zeigt soziale wie emotionale Intelligenz. Die Schule interessiert ihn nicht besonders, das Akademische schon gar nicht. Ganz im Gegensatz zu seinen Brüdern. Der eine ist heute promovierter Jurist, der jüngere, in Deutschland geborene, studiert noch. Anthony Sarpong weiß früh, dass er Koch werden will – auch wenn er zwischenzeitlich mal mit einer Fußballkarriere liebäugelt und sogar einen Fitnesstrainerschein macht. Seine Ausbildung in einem Wiesbadener Hotel hat er da bereits erfolgreich absolviert, er ist 19 Jahre alt.

»Ich wusste, was bei dem Job auf mich zukommt«, sagt Sarpong. Vor der Ausbildung hatte er Praktika in zwei Restaurants absolviert. »Bei einem habe ich gefühlt zwei Wochen nur an der Spüle gestanden, aber das hat mir nichts ausgemacht. Ich habe trotzdem viel gelernt.« Dennoch nimmt er sich nach der Lehre eine Auszeit. Als er dann ins Rhein-Main-Gebiet zurückkehrt, findet er sofort einen Job in Frankfurt. Von da an geht es mit seiner Karriere steil nach oben. Irgendwie hat sich das Talent des jungen Mannes herumgesprochen. Er kocht in Kasachstan, Spanien, Israel. Bis er irgendwann im Düsseldorfer Gourmet-Restaurant »Hummerstübchen« landet. Schon damals schaut er sich nach Räumen für ein eigenes Restaurant um. In Meerbusch wird er fündig.

MICHELIN-STARRED CHEF

"I believe in the dignity of all human beings. If you respect that, you'll be a happy person, yourself."

Anthony Sarpong has his parents to thank for many of the qualities that make him who he is today. His father's motto is 'live and let live' and this taught Sarpong tolerance and self-confidence. Meanwhile, his mother taught him the art of cooking. "In Ghana, cooking is a part of our culture. There's singing, there's dancing... the joie de vivre that comes with it is unbelievable," he explains. Born in Ghana in 1982, Sarpong is a Michelin-starred chef with his own restaurant in the Lower Rhine city of Meerbusch, as well as a father of three and an enthusiastic sportsman. In sum, he's a man who's happy and has achieved almost everything he's ever wished for. And he's "deeply at ease" with this. But this isn't just something Sarpong says about himself – everyone who meets him can sense it, too. He's known love from both his mother and his father, so Sarpong is a person who radiates warmth, friendliness and balance, and inspires them in all those around him.

In the late 80s, Sarpong's family decided to move to Germany. "It was important to my father that we learn something abroad," says the restaurateur. Indeed, his father was convinced that only those who were educated outside of Africa could ever gain recognition in the world. The family of four therefore moved to Wiesbaden and Sarpong's father found work at the local air base. Sarpong was placed into first-year classes speaking only a few words of German. He was the only Black student at the time, but that didn't bother him. He knew how to defend himself, including with his fists. Today, he's more diplomatic.

Even as a young boy, he was creative, fidgety and demonstrated social and emotional intelligence. He wasn't particularly interested in school, and especially not in academics. This makes him quite different from his brothers; one has a doctorate in law, while his younger brother, born in Germany, is still studying. Instead, Sarpong knew from an early age that he wanted to be a chef – despite having flirted with a football career at one time or another, and even qualifying as a fitness trainer.

By the age of nineteen, he'd already successfully completed his apprenticeship in a Wiesbaden hotel. "I knew what to expect with the job," Sarpong says. Before the apprenticeship, he completed internships at two restaurants: "At one, I felt like I'd spent two weeks just standing at the sink, but I didn't mind. I still learnt a great deal." Nevertheless, he decided to take some time off after his apprenticeship. When he later returned to the Rhine-Main area, he immediately found a job in Frankfurt. From then on, his career really took off. Word somehow got around about the young man's talent, and he went on to cook in Kazakhstan, Spain and Israel. Eventually, he touched down at

»Es war verrückt. Plötzlich war ich vom Koch zum Unternehmer geworden«, erinnert er sich. Die ganze Bürokratie, das Kaufmännische, damit kann er nichts anfangen. Das übernimmt seine Frau Birgül, die er liebevoll Bee nennt. »Mein Vater konnte den Namen Birgül nicht aussprechen, hat deswegen Bee gesagt, und seitdem nennen wir sie alle so«, erzählt Sarpong. Bee, Tochter türkischer Einwanderer, ist die Stütze des quirligen Kochs. »Für sie bin ich dankbar, ebenso für meine Kinder, die meine Frau zu so tollen Menschen erzogen hat.« Wenn Sarpong nicht in der Küche seines Restaurants steht, ist er mit seinen beiden Söhnen auf dem Fußballplatz, bringt seine Tochter zum Reiten oder verbringt Zeit mit seiner Frau im Garten.

Zu seinen größten Stärken zählt Sarpong, dass er sich immer wieder selbst motivieren könne, wenn es mal nicht so gut laufe, obwohl es bei ihm fast immer gut laufe. Auch »dummes Gerede« und Anfeindungen prallen an ihm ab. »Letztens hat mich jemand angerufen und mich beschimpft, auch weil ich ein Schwarzer bin. Ich habe ihn ausreden lassen und ihm dann gesagt, dass ich nun auflege«, erzählt der große, schlanke Mann und ist überzeugt, dass sich dieser Anrufer anschließend schlechter gefühlt hat als er. An ihm pralle das ab. Er schere sich nicht darum, was Menschen sagen, die ihm nicht nahestehen.

Sarpong ruht in sich. »Mir sind Status und Prominenz egal, auch was meine Gäste angeht. Das spüren und schätzen sie.« Sarpong ist nahbar, bei ihm sollen sich die Menschen wie zu Hause fühlen. Das habe er von seiner Mutter, die bis heute für alle kocht, wenn sie aus dem Rhein-Main-Gebiet in Meerbusch zu Besuch ist. Auch Neider lassen ihn kalt. Meist könnten oder wollten die seinen Erfolg als Schwarzer nicht glauben. »Rassismus ist eine Verletzung der Würde, und ich glaube an die Würde eines jeden Einzelnen, unabhängig von der Hautfarbe, der Religion, der Herkunft oder dem Geschlecht«, sagt er. Klar habe er als Kind auch mal dumme Sprüche zu hören bekommen und sich dann gewehrt. Seine Kinder aber würden wie selbstverständlich mit ihrer deutsch-afrikanisch-türkischen Herkunft leben. Sarpong sieht sich als Weltbürger, der keine kulturellen Grenzen kennt. Mit seiner Mutter spricht er einen einzigartigen Mix aus Deutsch, Englisch und Twi, der Sprache Ghanas.

Vorbilder oder Helden hat Sarpong nicht. Er sei jedoch voller Dankbarkeit, auch für seinen Erfolg und dass er in einem Land wie Deutschland leben könne. Davon wolle er etwas abgeben. »Ich habe inzwischen 18 Angestellte, für die habe ich eine Verantwortung.« Verantwortung übernimmt er auch für sein Heimatland. So hat er Anthony's Afrika Charity e. V. zur Förderung von Wirtschaft, Bildung und Gesundheit gegründet. Aktuelle Projekte sind etwa ein Ausbildungszentrum in Kumasi, eine Kochschule und ein Zentrum für Kinder-Unfallchirurgie.

»Ich mache, worauf ich Lust habe. Ich bin ein Freigeist«, sagt Sarpong und meint damit zunächst seinen Kochstil im Meerbuscher »Anthony's Kitchen«. Die Aussage treffe aber auch auf den ganzen Menschen Anthony Sarpong zu. Es sei eine Einstellung, die er vor allem seinen Eltern zu verdanken habe. Und so lautet sein Rat an sein zwölfjähriges Ich wie der Rat seines Vaters: »Leben und leben lassen.« Es ist diese Philosophie, die ihn zu dem Menschen gemacht hat, der er heute ist: glücklich, tolerant, gelassen und erfolgreich.

the Hummerstübchen gourmet restaurant in Düsseldorf. Even then, he was looking around for premises for his own restaurant. And he found what he was looking for in Meerbusch.

"It was crazy. Suddenly, I'd gone from being a chef to an entrepreneur," he recalls. All the bureaucracy, the commercial wrangling? He had no idea. His wife Birgül, whom he affectionately calls Bee, takes care of that for him. "My father couldn't pronounce the name Birgül, so he said Bee, and we've all called her that ever since!" Sarpong recounts. Bee, the daughter of Turkish immigrants, is the lively chef's rock: "I'm grateful for her and for my children, whom my wife has raised to be such great people." When Sarpong isn't in his restaurant's kitchen, he's out on the football field with his two sons, taking his daughter horse-riding, or spending time in the garden with his wife.

Sarpong believes one of his greatest strengths is that he can always motivate himself when things aren't going well, even though things are almost always going well for him. He also never gets hung up on "stupid talk" and hostility: "The other day someone phoned me and called me names, partly because I'm a Black man. I let him finish and then told him that I was hanging up on him," says the tall, slim man, who's convinced that the caller felt worse than he did afterwards. That kind of thing is like water off a duck's back to him. He doesn't care what's said by those not close to him.

Sarpong is at peace with himself: "I don't care about status and celebrity, even when it comes to my guests. They sense and appreciate that." The chef is approachable and wants people to feel at home. He says he got that from his mother who, to this day, cooks for everyone when she visits Meerbusch. Even envious people don't get to him; for the most part, people like this cannot or will not believe his success as a Black man. "Racism is a violation of dignity, and I believe in the dignity of every individual, regardless of skin colour, religion, origin or gender," he says. Of course, as a child he had to listen to stupid comments – and then he defended himself. But his children see their German-African-Turkish heritage as the most natural, normal thing in the world. Sarpong considers himself a global citizen and doesn't acknowledge cultural boundaries. Even with his mother, he speaks a unique blend of German, English and Twi, a Ghanaian language.

Sarpong has no role models or heroes. However, he's full of gratitude, including for his success and for the opportunity he was given to live in a country like Germany. Now he wants to pass that on: "I'm responsible for eighteen employees today." He also feels a certain responsibility towards his homeland. He therefore founded Anthony's Afrika Charity e.V. to promote business, health and education on the continent. The charity's current projects include a training centre in Kumasi, a cooking school, and a centre for paediatric trauma surgery.

"I do whatever I feel like doing. I'm a free spirit," says Sarpong, referring first and foremost to his style of cooking at Anthony's Kitchen in Meerbusch. But the statement also applies to Sarpong as a whole. It's an attitude he owes, above all, to his parents. And so, mirroring his own father's advice, he would tell his twelve-year-old self: "Live and let live." It's this philosophy that's made him the man he is today: successful, tolerant, calm and content.

Irene Appiah

BILDUNGSREFERENTIN

»Ich glaube, dass die Spiritualität dieser Welt in jedem von uns gebunden ist und dass wir aus eigener Stärke heraus Dinge bewegen können.«

Irene Appiah wartet nicht darauf, dass sich Dinge ändern, sondern sorgt selbst dafür. »Wo ich bin, bringe ich eine Veränderung hervor, weil ich das bin, was ich bin«, sagt die Juristin, die als Bildungsreferentin in der Hamburger Schulbehörde arbeitet. Als Studentin stellte sie sich in einer internationalen Kanzlei für Gesellschaftsrecht in Berlin vor – und wusste bereits beim Betreten des Foyers, dass sie den Job bekommen würde. Dem verdutzten Geschäftsführer erklärte Appiah, dass niemand eine internationale Gesellschaft besser repräsentieren könne als sie: Tochter ghanaischer Akademiker, in Hamburg geboren und aufgewachsen und mit exzellenten Englischkenntnissen. Selbstverständlich bekam sie den Job. »Ich akzeptiere nicht, dass ich etwas nicht bekomme, weil ich so aussehe, sondern drehe es für mich um: Ich bekomme etwas, weil ich so aussehe!«

In den 1970er-Jahren in einer Hochhaussiedlung im Hamburger Osten aufgewachsen, gehört Irene Appiah stets zu den ersten Schwarzen deutschen Mädchen: im Block und in der Schule, als Schulsprecherin, im Reitstall und im Handballverein. Sie staunt noch immer darüber, dass sie heute so selbstbewusst und »laut« sein könne. Als Jugendliche fand sie sich eher ruhig und beobachtend.

Dass Bildung Türen öffnet, begreift Irene Appiah bereits als 13-jährige Gesamtschülerin. Ihre Freundinnen kommen aus bürgerlichen weißen deutschen Familien. »Die Eltern hatten ein Problem damit, wo ich wohnte«, erinnert sie sich. »Aber weil ich klug war und gemeinsam mit ihren Kindern lernte, war ich bei ihnen zu Hause gern gesehen.« Ihr Vater, als Student politisch aktiv, vermittelt seinem einzigen Kind den Wert von Wissen und Bildung. Seine Tochter erzieht er zu einer selbstständigen Frau, die »nicht einfach so in das Haus eines Mannes zieht«. Beide stehen sich sehr nahe, sein Tod vor einigen Jahren lässt die Tochter endgültig erwachsen werden. »Ich vermisse ihn noch immer«, sagt sie. Ihre persönliche Heldin jedoch sei ihre Mutter, deren starken Willen sie bewundere. Aus sehr einfachen Verhältnissen stammend, hatte diese schon früh Geld verdient, um ihren Schulbesuch und den ihrer Geschwister zu bezahlen. Der jungen Irene gibt sie ihren Stolz mit und bestärkt sie immer wieder, sich gegen Hänseleien und Beleidigungen zu wehren. Ein persönliches Vorbild findet Irene als Jugendliche während der regelmäßigen Familienbesuche in den USA in der Moderatorin Oprah Winfrey. Deren Klugheit und Stärke bewundert sie bis heute.

Irene Appiah verabscheut Ungerechtigkeit und Benachteiligung und träumt bereits als Zehnjährige davon, Anwältin zu werden – damals eher »wegen der tollen Klamotten, die Anwältinnen in den US-Filmen trugen«, wie sie lachend erzählt. Dennoch verläuft ihr Lebensweg alles andere als geradlinig. Geprägt von der aufblühenden Hip-Hop-Szene in der Hansestadt – einer Zeit, die sie gern noch einmal erleben würde –, wird

EDUCATION OFFICER

"I believe that the spirituality of this world is bound up in each of us and that we can make things happen by virtue of our inner strength."

Irene Appiah doesn't wait for change; she pushes to make it happen. "I bring about change wherever I am because I am who I am," says the lawyer-turned-Hamburg School Authority education officer. As a student, she pictured herself working for an international commercial law firm in Berlin – and knew from the moment she crossed the threshold that she'd get the job. When the time came, Appiah explained to the stunned senior partner that no one could better represent an international business than her, the daughter of Ghanaian academics, born and raised in Hamburg, and boasting excellent English language skills. It goes without saying that she got the job: "I don't accept that I won't get something because I look the way I do. Instead, I turn it around: I'll get something *because* I look this way!"

Having grown up in a 70s high-rise in East Hamburg, Irene Appiah is used to being the first Black German girl: in the block, at school, as head girl, at the riding stables, and in the handball club. She's still amazed that she can be so self-confident and "loud" today; as a young girl, she was rather quiet and observant.

Enrolled at a comprehensive school, thirteen-year-old Appiah had already grasped that education opens doors. Her friends came from middle-class, white German families. "Their parents had a problem with where I lived," she remembers, "but because I was smart and went to school with their children, I was welcome in their home." Her father, who was politically active as a student, instilled in his only child the value of knowledge and education. His daughter thus grew into an independent woman who wouldn't end up "simply moving into another man's house". The pair were very close and her father's death a few years ago caused Appiah to grow up. "I still miss him," she says. However, her hero is her mother, whose strong will she greatly admires. Born into very modest circumstances, her mother started earning money at an early age to pay for herself and her siblings to attend school. She instilled a sense of pride in Irene and encouraged her again and again to defend herself against taunts and slurs. Young Irene discovered her personal role model on regular family visits to the US: TV host Oprah Winfrey. She remains impressed by her intelligence and strength to this day.

Appiah abhors injustice and discrimination and had dreamed of becoming a lawyer since she was ten – rather "because of the fabulous clothes that female lawyers wore in American movies at the time," she laughs. However, her life was destined to follow a very different path. Influenced by the burgeoning hip-hop scene in the Hanseatic city – a time she would love to relive – the student was booked as a background singer and dancer for the tours of international stars. After finishing school, she initially studied business, but the hip-hop

die Schülerin als Backgroundsängerin und Tänzerin für Tourneen internationaler Stars gebucht. Nach dem Abitur studiert sie zunächst Betriebswirtschaft, verbringt als Sängerin einer Hip-Hop-Band jedoch mehr Zeit in Clubs und Studios als im Hörsaal. Als die Karriere stockt, gründet sie eine Booking-Agentur für internationale Künstler und zieht nach Berlin. Irene Appiah ist Mitte 20, als sie sich auf ihre frühere Faszination für die Rechtswissenschaften besinnt und sich in Hamburg für ein Vollstudium einschreibt. Kurze Zeit später wird sie mit ihrem Sohn schwanger. Jurastudium und Berufstätigkeit bringen die bald alleinerziehende Mutter immer wieder an den Rand ihrer Kräfte. Denn: »Wenn ich etwas mache, dann richtig.«

Damit nicht genug. Gemeinsam mit einer befreundeten Anwältin gründet die Studentin einen Verein, der Hausaufgabenhilfe für Kinder mit Migrationshintergrund anbietet. Damit beginnt ihr ehrenamtliches Engagement für die Community, für das sie später von Bundespräsident Horst Köhler ausgezeichnet werden soll. Um die Familien bei der Kommunikation in Erziehungsfragen zu unterstützen, baut sie ein Netz von Sprach- und Kulturmittlern auf. Die junge Aktivistin besucht im Auftrag des Hamburger Senats Schulklassen, um Jugendliche zum Lernen zu motivieren. Später wird ihr die Leitung dieser Workshops angetragen. Bildung ist fortan ihr Herzensthema und zugleich ein Instrument, um ihrer Community »neue Wege zu zeigen«. Als Appiah ihr erstes Staatsexamen ablegt, ist sie bereits Mitarbeiterin der Hamburger Schulbehörde. Seitdem entwickelt sie als Bildungsreferentin interkulturelle Maßnahmen für Behörde und Schulen. Hier wird sie der »Lücken im Bildungssystem« gewahr und beschließt, in die Politik zu gehen. »In Hamburg leben viele Schwarze Kinder, aber wir haben keine Schwarzen Repräsentanten.« Sie will verändern – und dabei Vorbild sein.

Zynischerweise ist ihr Einstieg in die Politik von einer Rassismuserfahrung geprägt: Im Foyer der Parteizentrale wird sie von einer Mitarbeiterin zum Grundsicherungsamt ein paar Häuser weiter geschickt. Sie ist empört. »Dieses Bild in den Köpfen ist symptomatisch für diese Gesellschaft.« Doch sie wäre nicht Irene Appiah, hätte sie daraus nicht die Motivation gezogen, »genau dieses Bild zu verändern«. Was manche zum Aufgeben gebracht hätte, motiviert sie zu einem »Jetzt-erst-recht«. Mit den Stimmen aus der Community zieht Appiah in die Bezirksversammlung ein und übernimmt das Thema Jugendhilfe, später auch Soziales. Trotz des Erfolgs: Erfahrungen wie diese zehren an ihr. Auch deshalb verbindet sie mit ihrer Hautfarbe Stolz, aber auch Schmerz und Neid. »Als Schwarze Person erlebt man häufig Ablehnung und den Versuch, degradiert oder gebremst zu werden. Dinge, auf die man Anspruch hat, werden nicht ermöglicht, weil es bedeuten würde, unser Gegenüber müsste seinen Platz freigeben«, erzählt sie. Das sei schmerzhaft, »weil man meistens alleine damit fertig werden muss.« Deshalb beschreibt Irene Appiah Schwarze in Deutschland als »Mercedes mit Teslamotor«: »Man hat dieselben Qualitäten, muss jedoch deutlich mehr Gas geben, um dort hinzukommen, wo bereits jemand sitzt, der weniger aufwenden musste.« Aus diesen Erfahrungen habe sie gelernt. »In vielen Dingen, die ich umsetzen will oder muss, bin ich schneller und fitter. Ich bereite mich auf drei Situationen gleichzeitig vor.«

Auch deshalb weiß Irene Appiah, dass sie noch nicht am Ziel ist, dass noch Größeres auf sie wartet. Diese Lebenseinstellung würde sie auch ihrem zwölfjährigen Ich mitgeben: »Alles, was du machst oder lernst, hat einen Sinn. Hab keine Angst, dass du irgendwo rausfällst oder vom Weg abkommst. Wenn du deinem Gefühl vertraust, dann wirst du deinen Lebensweg finden.«

singer tended to spend more time in clubs and studios than in the lecture theatre. As her career faltered, she set up a booking agency for international artists and moved to Berlin. Then in her mid-20s, Appiah recalled her earlier fascination with the law and enrolled in a full-time degree at Hamburg Law School. A short while later, she became pregnant with her son. Studying law while holding down a job almost pushed the single mother over the edge because "when I do something, I do it right".

But she didn't stop there. Together with a lawyer friend, the student founded an association that offers children with an immigrant background help with their homework. Thus began her volunteer work for the community, for which she was later recognised by German Federal President Horst Köhler. In order to help families to communicate about educational matters, she built a network of language and cultural mediators. On behalf of the Hamburg Senate, the young activist also visited children in school to motivate them to learn. Later, she would take over running these workshops. Education has since been an issue dear to her heart, as well as a tool to help show her community "new possibilities". When Appiah sat her first state legal exam, she was already working for the Hamburg School Authority. In her role as Education Officer, she has since developed intercultural measures for authorities and schools. It was in doing this work that she became aware of "gaps in the education system" and decided to enter politics: "There are many Black children living in Hamburg, however, we have no Black representatives." She wanted to change that – and thus become a role model for them.

With a grim irony, her first experience of politics was marred by racism. In the foyer of the party headquarters, an employee tried to direct her a few doors down to the social security office. She was outraged: "This image in people's minds is symptomatic of this society." But she wouldn't be Irene Appiah if she hadn't been motivated by the experience to "change precisely this image". What would have made some give up motivated her to work even harder to achieve her goals. Votes from the community carried Appiah into the District Assembly, where she took over responsibility for youth services and, later, social welfare. Yet despite this success, experiences like this wear on her. This is another reason why she associates her skin colour with pride on one hand, and with pain and envy on the other: "As a Black person, you often experience rejection and people's attempts to degrade or slow you down. It's not always possible to get the things you're entitled to because it would mean that your counterpart would have to give up something of theirs," she explains. This is hurtful "because most of the time you have to deal with this alone". This is why Appiah describes Black people in Germany as "a Mercedes with a Tesla engine... you have the same qualities, but you have to step on the gas a lot harder to get to where someone else is already sitting without it having cost them as much." She admits that she's learnt from these experiences: "For many things I want or need to implement, I'm faster and fitter. I always prepare myself for three possible scenarios at once."

This is another reason why Appiah knows that she hasn't yet reached her end goal and that greater things are yet to come. She'd also share this mindset with her twelve-year-old self: "Everything that you do or learn has a purpose. Don't be scared that you'll somehow get lost or stray from your path. If you trust your gut, you'll find your way in life."

Kurz-Biografien / Short bios

Dayan Kodua

Dayan Kodua ist Schauspielerin, Sprecherin, Autorin und Gründerin des Gratitude Verlags. Geboren in Ghana und aufgewachsen in Kiel, folgte Dayan nach einem Abschluss als Wirtschaftsassistentin ihrem Herzen und studierte Schauspiel in Berlin und Los Angeles. Neben ihrer Arbeit als Schauspielerin und Sprecherin ist es ihr ein Anliegen, People of Color zu empowern und als Vorbilder sichtbarer zu machen. 2014 veröffentlichte sie deshalb den Bildband *My Black Skin: Schwarz. Erfolgreich. Deutsch* und rief dazu eine Wanderausstellung sowie entsprechende Workshops ins Leben. Besonders wichtig ist es Dayan, Kinder auf ihre innere Stärke aufmerksam machen. Diesem Thema widmet sie sich u. a. in ihren 2019 und 2021 erschienenen Bilderbüchern *Odo* und *Odo und der Beginn einer großen Reise*. Mit dem Gratitude Verlag möchte sie anderen Autorinnen und Autoren die Möglichkeiten geben, ihre diversen Geschichten der Öffentlichkeit zu präsentieren.

Dayan Kodua is an actress, speaker, author and founder of the Gratitude publishing company. Born in Ghana and raised in Kiel, Germany, Dayan initially trained as a business assistant. Then, she decided to follow her heart and studied acting in Berlin and Los Angeles. Alongside her work as an actress and speaker, she is passionate about empowering people of colour and lifting them up as role models. This is what prompted the 2014 publication of her illustrated book *My Black Skin: Schwarz. Erfolgreich. Deutsch,* which launched an associated touring exhibition and a series of workshops. It is especially important to Dayan to make children aware of their inner strength. Among other projects, she dedicated her 2019 and 2021 illustrated books, *Odo* and *Odo und der Beginn einer großen Reise* ('Odo and the Start of a Big Journey'), to this goal. Through the Gratitude publishing company, she would like to give other authors the opportunity to share their diverse stories with the world.

Thomas Leidig

In Lübeck geboren und aufgewachsen im Herzen Schleswig-Holsteins verschlug es Thomas Leidig Ende der 1980er für seine Fotografenausbildung nach Hamburg. Danach ging es weiter mit dem Studium der Angewandten Kulturwissenschaften in Lüneburg. Der Wahlhamburger porträtierte nationale und internationale Persönlichkeiten wie Mats Mikkelsen, Halle Berry, Christian Bale, Heike Makatsch, Jan Delay und viele mehr. In seinen reduzierten Inszenierungen konzentriert er sich immer auf den Menschen. Durch die Annäherung beim Shooting entstehen im wahrsten Sinne besondere und mitunter ironische Momentaufnahmen.

Thomas Leidig was born in Lübeck and raised in the heart of Schleswig-Holstein. After moving to Hamburg in the late 1980s to study photography, he continued his studies in applied cultural sciences in Lüneburg. Since then, many national and international stars have sat for the adoptive Hamburg resident, including Mads Mikkelsen, Halle Berry, Christian Bale, Heike Makatsch, and Jan Delay. Leidig focuses solely on the person in front of his lens with his signature minimalist style, an approach that produces genuinely striking and somewhat dramatic shots.

Susanne Dorn

Susanne Dorn absolvierte nach dem Studium der Betriebswirtschaftslehre ein PR-Volontariat. Anschließend arbeitete die gebürtige Hamburgerin mehrere Jahre als Lokalreporterin beim *Hamburger Abendblatt* und als Online-Redakteurin bei der Verlagsgruppe Milchstraße. Mittlerweile ist sie wieder im PR-Bereich tätig und zeichnet u. a. für die Website, Ausstellungen und Publikationen der Arbeitsgemeinschaft selbstständiger Migranten e. V. (ASM) verantwortlich. Susanne Dorn ist die Autorin des ersten Bandes *My Black Skin – Schwarz. Erfolgreich. Deutsch,* den Dayan Kodua 2014 herausgegeben hat. »Ich habe großen Respekt vor der Lebensleistung der von mir Porträtierten. Mich hat die Arbeit an den beiden Bänden bereichert, und ich bin dankbar für die Offenheit, mit der mir meine Interviewpartnerinnen und -partner begegnet sind.«

After graduating from business school, Susanne Dorn completed an internship in PR. The native Hamburg resident then spent several years working as a local reporter for evening paper *Hamburg Abendblatt* and as an online editor for the Milchstraße publishing group. In time, she returned to her PR roots and is now responsible, among other things, for the website, exhibitions and publications of the German Association of Self-Employed Migrants (Arbeitsgemeinschaft selbstständiger Migranten e. V.). Dorn is the author of the first book in the *My Black Skin* series, *Schwarz. Erfolgreich. Deutsch.*, which was published by Dayan Kodua in 2014. "I have an enormous respect for what the people I interviewed have achieved in their lives. I found it deeply rewarding to work on these two volumes and am grateful for the candour with which my interviewees approached our meetings."

Hat interviewt / She interviewed:
Prof. Dr. Marylyn Addo
Vivian Abena Ansuhenne
Akosua Ina'mi Aset
Gloria Boateng
Thilo Cablitz
Dr. Karamba Diaby
Saliya Kahawatte
Delaine Pastor Kühn
Dr. Stephanie Nsiah-Dosu
Adelaide Wolters

Britta Schmeis

Britta Schmeis, 1972 in Hilden bei Düsseldorf geboren und aufgewachsen, studierte Amerikanistik und Betriebswirtschaftslehre in Hamburg. Anschließend volontierte sie bei der Deutschen Presse-Agentur. Seitdem arbeitet sie als freie Journalistin und Autorin mit den Schwerpunkten Film, Literatur und Gesellschaft unter anderem für *Die Welt/Welt am Sonntag, Spiegel online* und *epd Film*. Sie möchte Menschen eine Stimme geben, die sonst kaum gehört werden und von Leben erzählen, die für viele völlig fremd sind, um so den Blick für die Vielfalt unserer Welt zu öffnen. Britta Schmeis hat eine Tochter und lebt mit ihrer Familie in Hamburg.

Born in 1972 and raised in Hilden near Düsseldorf, Britta Schmeis has a degree in American Studies and Business from Hamburg University. After graduating, she volunteered with the German Press Agency (*dpa*). She has since built a career as a freelance journalist and author specialising in film, literature and society for publications such as *Die Welt/Welt am Sonntag, Spiegel Online* and *epd Film*. She wants to give a voice to those who are rarely heard and share the stories of those whose lives are, to many, completely foreign. In doing so, she hopes to open our eyes to the diversity our world has to offer. Schmeis has a daughter and lives with her family in Hamburg.

Hat interviewt / She interviewed:
Arrey Kono Enow
Prof. Dr. Thomas Kapapa
Stephania Mbianda
Paguiel Mlapa
Dr. Akuma Saningong
Anthony Sarpong
Daniel & Adrian Sousa

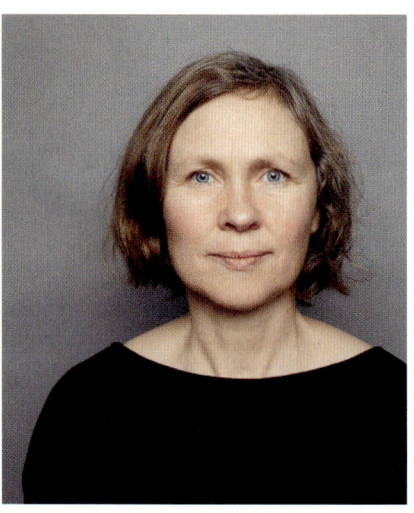

Michaela Ludwig

Michaela Ludwig arbeitete nach ihrem Studium der Neueren deutschen Literatur und Soziologie und Praktika bei den *Lübecker Nachrichten* und der *Hamburger Morgenpost* als Redakteurin für eine Hamburger Fernsehproduktionsgesellschaft. Seit einem Volunteer-Aufenthalt in Uganda schreibt die gebürtige Schleswig-Holsteinerin für Zeitungen, Magazine und Nichtregierungsorganisationen. Als Partnerin bei agenda fotografen & journalisten recherchierte sie Reportagen und Features in Hamburg und der Welt. Heute ist sie hauptsächlich im PR-Bereich tätig und schreibt über Themen aus Arbeitswelt und Bildung. Begeistert ist sie von den Begegnungen mit unterschiedlichsten Menschen und dem Eintauchen in deren Lebenswelten. Sie möchte ihnen die Möglichkeit geben, ihre Geschichten zu erzählen und ihre Sicht auf die Welt darzustellen.

After studying modern German literature and sociology – and completing internships with newspapers *Lübecker Nachrichten* and *Hamburger Morgenpost* – Michaela Ludwig secured employment as an editor for a Hamburg television production company. Following a stint as a volunteer in Uganda, the native German from Schleswig-Holstein wrote for a variety of newspapers, magazines and NGOs. As a partner at *agenda fotografen & journalisten,* she also researched reports and features in Hamburg and around the globe. Today, Wolters works mainly in PR and writes about topics from the world of work and education. She delights in meeting as many different people as possible and immersing herself in their lives. She wants to give them the opportunity to tell their stories and share their worldviews with others.

Hat interviewt / She interviewed:
Samuel Agyapong
Irene Appiah
Bradley Iyamu
Joana Kohrs
Enoch Wölfer

Moira Monney

Moira Monney, 1982 in Gütersloh geboren und aufgewachsen, ist die Tochter eines Schwarzen Vaters und einer weißen Mutter. Nach ihrem Studium der Angewandten Sprachen mit Wirtschaft und Recht in Paris, Frankreich, ging sie nach England und war dort zunächst als Marketing Executive und dann als Key Account Managerin in der Foodbranche tätig. Seit 2007 ist sie als freie Übersetzerin und Texterin tätig. Ihr Unternehmen NEM Content Marketing unterstützt Firmen im Bereich Ernährung/Nahrungsergänzungsmittel (NEM). 2019 initiierte Moira Monney die Onlinekonferenz Financial Success Summit for Translators und bietet seitdem Training und Coaching für Übersetzerkolleginnen und -kollegen an. »Ich freue mich, wenn ich anderen Schwarzen und braunen Menschen zu mehr Sichtbarkeit verhelfen kann und fühle mich geehrt, dass ich an diesem tollen Projekt mitwirken durfte.«

Born in 1982 and raised in Gütersloh, Germany, Moira Monney is the bilingual daughter of a Black father and a white mother. After studying Applied Languages with Business and Law in Paris, she moved to England where she worked in the food industry, first as a marketing executive and later as a key account manager. She's been a freelance translator and copywriter since 2007, and her company, NEM Content Marketing, serves businesses working in the food and nutrition sector. In 2019, Monney launched the online Financial Success Summit for Translators, and has since offered regular training and coaching to her translation colleagues. "I love helping to raise the visibility of other Black and brown people and feel honoured to have contributed to this wonderful project."

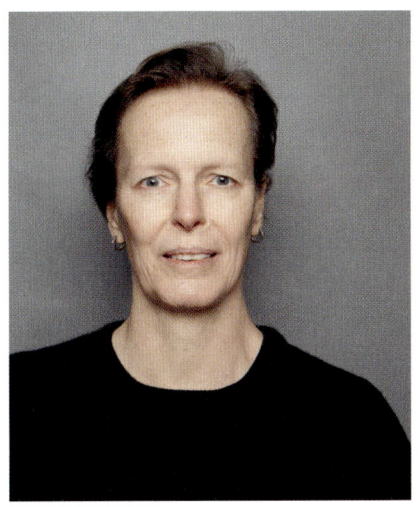

Marie Jackson

Marie Jackson wurde 1990 in der britischen Küstenstadt Portsmouth geboren. Schon seit ihrem vierten Lebensjahr liebt sie Sprachen. Während ihres Dolmetsch- und Übersetzungsstudiums in Schottland zog es sie immer wieder ins Ausland, unter anderem lebte sie in Innsbruck und Paris. Nach ihrem Abschluss unterrichtete sie an einer weiterführenden Schule im österreichischen Klagenfurt. 2012 begann Marie mit der Gründung von Looking-Glass Translations ihre Karriere als Übersetzerin und Redakteurin, spezialisiert auf Wirtschaft, Marketing und Recht. 2018 zog es Marie erneut in die Fremde, diesmal ins niederländische Tilburg, wo sie ihre akademische Laufbahn um einen Bachelor-Abschluss in internationalem Recht erweiterte. Heute lebt und arbeitet Marie Jackson im schottischen Edinburgh. Ihre Kunden sind Unternehmer und Firmen im Rechtsbereich, zudem unterstützt sie die ortsansässige Zweigstelle einer internationalen Menschenrechtsorganisation. Sie ist sehr stolz auf ihr spanisch-jamaikanisches Erbe und bezeichnet es als Ehre, an einem Projekt mitgewirkt zu haben, das die Schwarze Community feiert.

Born in 1990 in the British coastal city of Portsmouth, Marie Jackson has adored languages since the age of four. After studying interpreting and translation in Scotland, prompting moves to Innsbruck and Paris, she enjoyed a stint teaching at a secondary school in Klagenfurt, Austria. She founded Looking-Glass Translations in 2012 and has since built a career as a translator and editor in business, marketing and law. In 2018, she moved abroad again to Tilburg, the Netherlands, to complete an LLB in Global Law. Jackson now lives in Edinburgh, Scotland, where she serves a mixture of business and legal clients, and assists the local branch of an international human rights charity. She's very proud of her Jamaican-Spanish heritage and considers it the honour of her career to have contributed directly to a project that lifts up her community.

Katja Ernst

1966 in Bremen geboren, absolvierte Katja Ernst nach einem einjährigen Aufenthalt in Oxford, England, eine Ausbildung zur Verlagskauffrau und studierte Germanistik und Geschichte in Düsseldorf und Hamburg. Danach war sie in verschiedenen Buchverlagen bzw. literarischen Agenturen beschäftigt. Zu ihren Arbeitgebern gehörten die Econ Verlagsgruppe, die Agentur Liepman in Zürich sowie die Verlage Rowohlt und Delius Klasing. Heute arbeitet sie als freie Lektorin und Übersetzerin in Hamburg.

Born in Bremen in 1966, Katja Ernst spent a year in Oxford, UK, before training as a publishing agent and studying German language, literature and history in Düsseldorf and Hamburg. After graduating, she worked for a myriad of publishing houses and literary agencies. Her employers have included the Econ publishing group, the Liepman agency in Zurich, and the publishers Rowohlt and Delius Klasing. Today, she works as a freelance translator and proofreader in Hamburg.

Danksagung

Es gibt Menschen, die dir etwas sagen, ohne zu wissen, dass sie dich damit in die richtige Richtung lenken. Ich möchte mich für all diese wunderbaren Begegnungen bedanken!

Ich danke den Menschen, die mich begleitet und gut beraten, mir Tipps und Hinweise gegeben haben. Denen, die mit mir an das Projekt *My Black Skin: Lebensreisen* geglaubt und mir Mut gemacht haben, weiter daran zu arbeiten. Danke an mein großartiges Team. Ohne euch wäre das alles nicht möglich gewesen. Man braucht einander, um im Leben Ziele zu erreichen.

Ich danke meinem fantastischen Mann Steffen! Danke, dass du mich bei allem, was ich mache, immer von ganzem Herzen und mit aller Kraft unterstützt. Vielen Dank an meine Schwester Cherine, dass du so bist, wie du bist. Mama und Dad, ich danke euch, denn ohne eure Heldenreise, euren Mut, von Ghana nach Kiel auszuwandern und bei null zu beginnen, wäre ich nicht die Person, die ich heute sein darf!

Dankeschön. Ich liebe euch.

Acknowledgements

There are people who say things to you without realising they are steering you in the right direction. I am grateful for all of these wonderful encounters!

Thank you to all of the people who have helped me, given me good advice, and shared their hints and tips – it is you who believed in the *My Black Skin: A Journey Through Life* project and encouraged me to keep working on it. Thank you also to my incredible team. Without you, none of this would have been possible. We are living proof that it takes a village to achieve our goals in life.

I would also like to express thanks to my fantastic husband, Steffen! Thank you for so completely and wholeheartedly supporting everything I do. Thank you so much to my sister, Cherine, for being who you are. Mama and Dad, I am grateful to you because without your own hero's journeys – and without the courage it took to start over when you moved from Ghana to Kiel – I wouldn't be the person I am today.

Thank you! I love you.

Das Projekt *My Black Skin* wurde 2013 von Dayan Kodua initiiert. 2014 erschien *My Black Skin: Schwarz. Erfolgreich. Deutsch.* *My Black Skin: Lebensreisen* ist der zweite Teil.

The *My Black Skin* project was launched by Dayan Kodua in 2013. The first book in the series, *My Black Skin: Schwarz. Erfolgreich. Deutsch.*, was published in 2014. *My Black Skin: A Journey Through Life* is the second illustrated volume.

Herausgeberin / Publishing:
Dayan Kodua, www.dayan-k.de

Fotografie / Photography:
Thomas Leidig, www.thomasleidig.de

Art Direction:
Julia Wagner, www.grafikanstalt.com

Deutsche Texte / Original German Text:
Susanne Dorn, Michaele Ludwig, Britta Schmeis

Lektorat / German Copy Editing:
Katja Ernst, www.lektorat-hamburg.net

Englische Übersetzung / English Translation:
Moira Monney, www.nemcontentmarketing.de
Marie Jackson, www.lookingglasstranslations.com

Druck und Buchbinderei / Printing and binding:
Livonia Print SIA

Erschienen im / Published by:
Gratitude Verlag
Lohmühlenstrasse 1
20099 Hamburg
Deutschland / Germany
Tel.: +49 40 86 68 22 81
Mob.: +49 172 415 77 66
www.gratitudeverlag.de

1. Auflage / First edition

© 2022 Gratitude Verlag, Hamburg, und Autoren / and authors

© 2022 für die abgebildeten Werke von / for featured works by Thomas Leidig: der Künstler / the artist

Printed in Europe

ISBN: 978-3-98207-686-7

Umschlagabbildung / Cover illustration: Irene Appiah, 2021

Presseanfragen an / Press enquiries:
Deutschmann Kommunikation
Nina Deutschmann
Tel.: +49 40 386 77 360
E-Mail / Email: info@deutschmann-kommunikation.de

Alle Rechte vorbehalten.

All rights reserved.

Dieses Buch darf nur nach vorheriger schriftlicher Zustimmung des Copyrightinhabers vollständig bzw. teilweise vervielfältigt, in einem Datenerfassungssystem gespeichert oder mit elektronischen bzw. mechanischen Hilfsmitteln, Fotokopierern oder Aufzeichnungsgeräten oder anderweitig verarbeitet werden.

No part of this publication may be reproduced, stored in a retrieval system, or transmitted in any form or by any means, electronic, mechanical, photocopying, recording or otherwise, without the prior written permission of the copyright holder.

Alternative Streitbeilegung gemäß Art. 14 Abs. 1 ODR-VO und § 36 VSBG:

Die Europäische Kommission stellt eine Plattform zur Online-Streitbeilegung (OS) bereit, die du unter https://ec.europa.eu/consumers/odr findest. Zur Teilnahme an einem Streitbeilegungsverfahren vor einer Verbraucherschlichtungsstelle sind wir nicht verpflichtet und nicht bereit.

Alternative dispute resolution in accordance with Art. 14(1) of the European Online Dispute Resolution Regulation and Art. 36 of the German Act on Alternative Dispute Resolution in Consumer Matters:

The European Commission provides an online dispute resolution (ODR) platform at https://ec.europa.eu/consumers/odr. We are neither willing nor obliged to participate in a dispute resolution procedure before a consumer arbitration board.

Wir bedanken uns für die freundliche Unterstützung:

WHITE & CASE